C000175609

Moray Sp

A TRAVEL GUIDE

Iona Grant

1st Edition

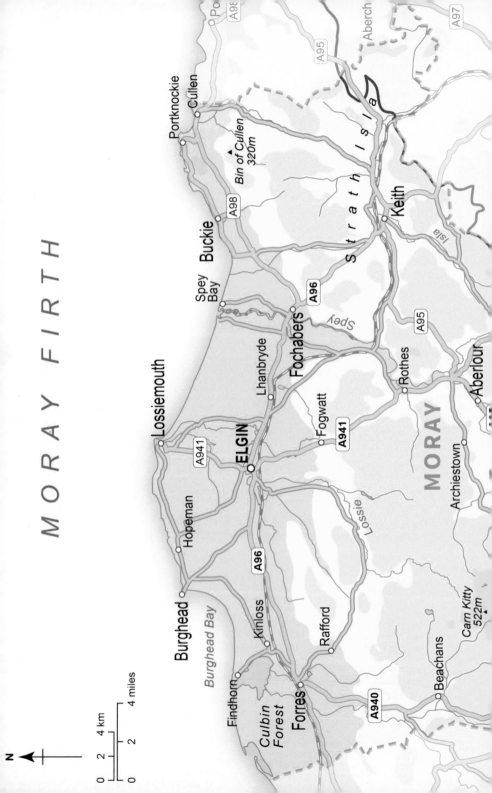

From Coast: 1 A dolphin breaches near Spey Bay wildlife reserve. **2** Take a tour of Covesea Lighthouse, Lossiemouth. **3** Discover the charming fishing village of Findochty.

To Countryside: 1 Infinite views are reflected in *Still*, Tomintoul. **2** Encounter the iconic Craigellachie Bridge across the famous River Spey. **3** The Divie Viaduct cuts through the landscape on the Dava Way walk.

Family days out: 1 Enjoy one of many organised activities as a family with Outfit Moray, or let the kids join in with a group of other youngsters. **2** Meet the friendly water buffalo at Thorabella Farm near Dallas. **3** Spey Bay is one of the best locations in Moray for dolphin spotting – learn all about these intelligent creatures at the Scottish Dolphin Centre and Tugnet Icehouse. **4** Get hands-on with helicopters and military jets at Morayvia, Kinloss. **5** Discover the magical Fairy Village near Dufftown. **6** The Elgin Reptile is even older than the dinosaurs! Find out more at the Elgin Museum.

3

4

5

6

The Great Outdoors: 1 Take a trip with North 58° Sea Adventures for close encounters with marine wildlife including dolphins and seals. **2** Beaches and estuaries are excellent for many water sports, including kite-surfing. **3** Climb a Corbett – Ben Rinnes is the highest peak in Moray and commands views over seven counties.

AUTHOR

Iona grew up in Burghead on the Moray Coast, where she was a keen member of numerous amateur dramatic societies and orchestral groups. She studied at Lossiemouth High School before going on to earn a media degree. After university Iona found herself adventure-bound for several years on cruise ships. Now safely back on land, she enjoys motorbiking, photography and playing trumpet.

AUTHOR'S STORY

Moray is one of the best-kept secrets in UK travel and in the summer of 2020, I spent a month visiting my family in Burghead.

The warm summer sun fuelled my desire for adventure as I grabbed Dad's squeaky bike from the shed and pedalled out of the village.

My fitness levels didn't match my enthusiasm, but I made it as far as Findhorn, riding the wide tracks of the Burma Road through the Roseisle forest, and then along the coastal trail above the pale dunes of the bay. I picked up lunch from the café at the Findhorn Foundation, admiring their eco-village along the way, and then parked my bike down by the estuary, enjoying the views across this important wildlife reserve.

My route back to Burghead took me to the beautiful ruins of medieval Kinloss Abbey and I finally made it back to my parents' house very tired, and very happy.

I spent many more days out exploring the nearby villages by bike, or taking the car and heading further east for to the picturesque fishing villages such as Cullen with its stunning viaduct.

I journied south to the hills of whisky country to climb the heathery mass of Ben Rinnes, Moray's highest peak, and visit the cool waters below the double cascades of the Falls of Linn of Ruthrie, near Aberlour

My month was over all too quick, and I headed home with a head full of happy memories which have inspired this guide book.

I hope it will help you to create some wonderful memories of your own.

ACKNOWLDEGEMENTS

I couldn't have done this without the endless cups of tea from my husband Robbie; or my parents who joined me on many days out. All the people who generously gave their time to chat, read, review and support me along the way including Sir Guy Macpherson-Grant, Elgin Museum, the Scottish Dolphin Centre, Outfit Moray, North 58°, Graham Gordon, Georgina Westley, John Gray, Brian Cameron, Ed Dunbar, and Emily Eastburn-Pentreath.

MORAY SPEYSIDE ONLINE
For additional content, articles, accommodation, dining and more on Moray Speyside, visit ⦾morayspeyside.com

First edition published November 2021
1ˢᵗ repint December 2021
IGB Publishing
2 Barnwood Close, Ruislip HA4 7HE
www.igb-publishing-yolasite.com
Text copyright © 2021 Iona Grant
Maps copyright © 2021 IGB Publishing; includes map data © OpenStreetMap contributors
Photographs copyright © 2021 Iona Grant and individual photographers, and also those from picture libraries credited beside images

Front cover by Georgina Westley
Back cover Dolphins at Burghead © North 58°
Title page Ballindalloch Castle © Ballindalloch Trust
Burghead Sands lyrics © Gordon Menzies, Gaberlunzie
Book design by Iona Grant
Maps David McCutcheon FBCart.S

Production managed by Jellyfish Print Solutions; printed in the UK

ISBN 9781838480202
British Library Cataloguing in Publication Data
A catalogue record for this book is available from the British Library

CONTENTS

Enjoy Moray Speyside

The burr of the local Scots dialect known as The Doric can be heard across Moray and Aberdeenshire, getting stronger the further east you travel. It is an old language of farming and fishing folk and whilst you won't hear broad Doric spoken so much these days, many words are still in everyday use.

Moray is full of stunning scenery, wildlife and history. *National Geographic* named the Moray coastline as one of the top twelve of the world's most beautiful and unspoiled coastlines.

The region is home to more than 50 whisky distilleries – that's nearly half of the distilleries in the whole of Scotland, concentrated in one amazing area.

Moray has escaped mass tourism – most of those who want a taste of Scotland might spend a few days in Edinburgh followed by a brief fling in the Highlands. Little do they know that they are missing out on some of the best weather, and most diverse landscapes. From the remote Scalan Seminary in The Cabrach, to the ancient forests and fast-flowing rivers of Speyside, historic towns of the Laich and the charming fishing villages along the coast, there is much beauty and history to discover.

Across Moray, traditional Highland games are held throughout the summer months – more than just an athletic event where you can cheer on strongmen as they toss the caber, the Highland games are awash with tartan: skirlin' pipe bands perform in all their finery, whilst whirling kilted dancers compete to execute the best Highland Fling and Sword Dance. Talented artisans showcase their wares, alongside purveyors of fine local produce on the busy market stalls at many events. The friendly people who live in Moray welcome visitors to join in their Highland Games, new year celebrations and festivals of music, food, and drink.

Tomintoul, nestled on the northern slopes of the Cairngorms, has recently been awarded Dark Skies Park status. High altitude and low levels of light pollution make it a great spot for observing the northern lights and other astronomical events. As the highest village in the Highlands, Tomintoul makes a perfect base for exploring the mountains year round, and in winter you can take part in snow-sports at the nearby Lecht ski resort.

Come down from Tomintoul and into the other villages of the Spey Valley, to enjoy waterfalls, salmon rivers and some of the picturesque distilleries on the Malt Whisky Trail.

East of the mouth of the Spey are beautiful beaches of soft pale sand, and pretty little fishing villages, where the colourful tradition of painting the stones of your cottage is very much in evidence. Stop off in Cullen and tuck into a bowl of Cullen Skink – a local delicacy of creamy smoked haddock soup.

West of Speyside, you come to the Laich O' Moray, with its rolling farmland stretching all the way to the sea, and stunning cathedrals and abbeys from the Middle Ages.

Being a responsible tourist is very much about balance. Just enough visitors to boost the economy, but no more than the infrastructure can handle. You still want to feel that your experience is unique, and you aren't being funnelled into the next big tourist attraction. So many of the wonderful attractions in Moray are free or have a such an incredibly low entrance charge that it feels rude not to spend a little more money. Treat yourself to a 'fly-cup and a fancy piece,' (as they say in Moray), at the café, or buy a beautiful souvenir from the giftshop. Maybe you'd like to drop a bit more cash in their donation box.

Stay local, shop local. Create memories, take photographs, leave footprints – and maybe a piece of your heart.

Aspects of Moray
A HISTORY OF THE SHIRE

Moray has a long and rich history, with the populations leaving traces of their existence behind them.

Before the dinosaurs, ancient reptiles lived on the red sands near Hopeman and left tell-tale tracks imprinted in the land. Stone Age settlers left flint arrows and spearheads at Culbin, and Bronze Age tools have been found in other parts of the county, showing how densely populated it was.

In the 4th century, the Picts made Moray their home for several hundred years. They established a great wooden fort at Burghead and evidence of their art and holy places can be found from the coast to the foot of the Cairngorms.

Great battles were fought against Vikings including the Battle for Mortlach near Dufftown in 1010, and the Battle of Torfness when it is considered that Jarl Thorfin the Mighty of Orkney, sought to capture the Pictish fort at Burghead in 1040.

Medieval Moray was ruled by Mormaers (a semi-royal status akin to being an earl) and covered a greater area than it does today. It stood apart from the Kingdom of Scotland until Macbeth of Shakespearean infamy came along. Macbeth would have been mormaer in 1034. His coronation as King of Scotland in 1040 united Moray with the rest of the Scottish kingdom.

The Dark Ages were turbulent times in Scotland. Whilst the 12th century saw education and growth as exemplified by the construction of Kinloss Abbey, the death of Alexander III in 1286 left the county without a monarch.

Edward I of England was asked to help prevent a civil war and so he crowned John Balliol, who was very much a puppet king until Edward insisted

Balliol sent troops to help England fight against France. Instead, Balliol signed a mutual defence pact with France. Edward responded by conquering Scotland, throwing Balliol in the Tower of London, and taking the Stone of Scone to Westminster Abbey.

Resistance and rebellion came from Andrew Murray in the north of Scotland, and William Wallace in the south. Murray gave the order to burn Duffus Castle which was owned by a supporter of Edward. Andrew Murray, the last mormaer of Moray died at the battle of Stirling Bridge in 1297.

Wallace was executed in 1305, and in the following year Robert the Bruce made his move and became King of Scotland.

The **Wolf of Badenoch** was the grandson of Robert the Bruce. The nickname was given posthumously to Alexander Stewart for his destruction of much of Elgin, in particular the cathedral. A feud between The Wolf and the Bishop of Moray developed from the bishop's refusal to annul Stewart's marriage so that he could wed his mistress. As well as torching Elgin and its cathedral, Stewart also set fire to many buildings in Forres and the abbey at Pluscarden.

The Scottish Enlightenment of the 1700s saw the lives of the poor in Moray change for the better. Loch Spynie was drained to reveal rich fertile farmlands. From the Cairngorms to the coast, villages and towns were established or improved by the introduction of new harbours, broad streets and town squares, new housing and sanitation.

By contrast, during the Highland clearances of 1750-1860, crofters were forcibly displaced from their farmlands to make way for large-scale sheep farming by the Duke and Duchess of Sutherland. Villages were set on fire – sometimes with people still in their homes if they refused or were unable to move. An estimated 6,000 Highlanders died. Of those who survived, approximately 70,000 emigrated to North America – some chose to go whilst others were forced or even sold as indentured slaves. Instrumental in facilitating the evictions were William Young and Patrick Sellar who were factors to the Sutherlands. Young founded Hopeman and Burghead (the latter in partnership with Sellar), benefitting from the displaced crofters.

For centuries, fishing has been an important source of employment in Moray. In the early 1900s, Buckie was the major fishing port in Moray, and despite their size, many of the smaller villages were also important fishing ports, landing catches of cod, herring, and haddock. Early forms of commercial fishing were labour intensive, and trawling was introduced in the late 19th century. The arrival of the railways in the 1850s meant that fresh fish could reach new markets – and just about every town and village was connected by branch lines connecting to the main railway between Aberdeen and Inverness.

The fishing industry was seriously affected by World Wars I and II. Post-war, over-fishing led to a decline in fish stocks, but under the EU's Common Fisheries Policy, cod stocks in the Scottish waters of the North Sea are once again sustainable. Fishing in Moray continues on a small scale and many of the harbours are now welcome ports for pleasure boats and water-based leisure activities.

Today, the three main products of Moray are timber, livestock, and whisky. With the current desire for sustainable business models, the three complement each other: woodchip is used to provide heat for distilling malted barley into whisky, and a by-product of distillation is used as a livestock feed.

The Muckle Spate

The Muckle Spate was a natural disaster which affected much of Moray in 1829 and remains one of the most momentous events in the long history of the county.

The summer of '29 had been exceptionally dry. On the evening of Saturday the 1st of August, a large black cloud gathered over the Moray Firth, growing larger and darker as night drew in. The ominous dark mass moved south over the Laich but didn't break until it reached the peaks of the Monadhliath mountains to the west of Kingussie.

Early on the Sunday morning the rain burst down on to the hillsides, with torrents of water rushing down every channel. The small streams that formed the tributaries of the Findhorn and Nairn became tumbling torrents.

The rains which poured down incessantly all of Monday and Tuesday were accompanied by a violent north-east wind and the deluge spread in all directions.

The waters of the main rivers, being the Findhorn, Spey, Lossie, and Nairn, rose to unprecedented heights, spreading devastation and terror as they swept across the country and out to sea – a flood stone near Randolph's Leap marks the greatest height of the flood.

The noise of the event was incredible: great rocks from the riverbeds crashed down the valleys; buildings, trees, and strong stone bridges were destroyed and joined with the debris being forced towards the Moray Firth.

At the mouth of the Spey, Garmouth and Kingston were in danger of being completely destroyed as the rolling tide, fuelled by the gale-force winds, increased to mountainous waves and threatened to destroy the villages.

When day broke on the 4th, the climax of the storm had passed and there were scenes of utter desolation. From the vantage point of Castlehill in Forres, floodwaters stretched as far west as the eye could see, and all the way to Findhorn where boats from the fishing village were able to carefully sail across submerged farmland to rescue terrified householders from the roofs of their homes. The town of Elgin appeared to be an island as hundreds of acres of low-lying land surround it were underwater, and reclaimed Loch Spynie was temporarily restored.

In all, 22 bridges and 60 houses were destroyed. Although only eight people lost their lives, 600 families were made homeless. Destitution followed, and many farmers and householders faced ruin although this was partially averted by relief funds.

THE MAGIC OF MORAY

Nestled in the rain shadow of the Grampian Hills, Moray is sunnier and drier than other regions of Scotland, as it benefits from the warmth of the Gulf Stream and the shelter of mountain ranges. Summer days are long, and the nights are light as the sun sets late in the evening – at about 10.30pm on Midsummer's Eve.

The Scottish dolphin is about 30% larger than its Caribbean cousin, a characteristic that helps keep them warm in the northern waters: nearly 200 dolphins swim in the bay of the Moray Firth. Red squirrels and pine martens live in the forests, and osprey fish for salmon in the rivers.

Moray falls naturally into three easily identifiable sections: The Laich o' Moray, Speyside, and the east.

In the west, the Laich o' Moray ("laich" being an old Scots word that describes a flattish, low-lying area of fertile farmlands) contains the coast trail from Findhorn to Lossiemouth, and the main towns and villages in the arable lands from Brodie, through to Fochabers.

The River Spey forms a natural break in the region's geography. From its source in the grey Monadhliath Mountains which flank the north-west of the Cairngorms, to the Moray Firth, the towns and villages along the banks of the fast flowing Spey, make up Speyside.

On the northern slopes of the Cairngorms, Tomintoul is said to be the highest village in the Highlands, where the hills form part of Moray. From Tomintoul, to Keith in the Isla Valley, lies the rich heritage of whisky distilleries.

East Moray doesn't have a local name, but the pretty fishing villages have enough charm that they don't need branding.

HIGHLAND GAMES

Scotland has a long history of Highland games, and they are often the highlight of a visit for many people. There is a tradition that clan chiefs held contests as long ago as the 11th century to find their fastest runners and toughest fighting men. The chief's requirements were not just for war, he also needed talented musicians and dancers for entertainment. This formed the basis of the games as we know them today. The modern Highland games are devoted to preserving and promoting Scottish culture at its best. In Moray, the games are often the main highlight of the year and the focus of community life.

Many events at the Highland games use items which could have been part of everyday life. Shot-puts were probably originally round stones from riverbeds, and a roughly trimmed Scots pine trunk is still the caber as is tossed today.

In recent years, crowds of 5,000 people from around the world have attended some of the games in Moray, proving the popularity of these events. Locals and visitors mingle throughout the day, enjoying Highland dancing, bagpiping, and drumming competitions, and heavy events (as caber tossing and hurling are known). It's also a great opportunity to buy from local artists and food producers as they show off their own skills in the busy market stalls.

MORAY AND THE MILITARY

Moray has a long association with the British military services. The fortunes of Kinloss and Lossiemouth are closely associated with the British military.

In 1939, an RAF station was established at Kinloss as a training base, and barracks were constructed. In post-war Britain, the station at Kinloss was under the control of Coastal Command – a division of the RAF which had been responsible for providing airborne protection for maritime activities during the war, monitored Russian ships and submarines in the Norwegian Sea.

The RAF's fleet of maritime patrol Nimrods remained at Kinloss until 2010 but changes to the UK's defence policy resulted in RAF Kinloss becoming surplus to requirements. Regular flying operations ceased in July 2011 and the base was abandoned by RAF personnel, although the landing strips continued to be used by RAF Lossiemouth.

Since 2012 the barracks at former RAF Kinloss have been home to the British Army's Military Engineers, 39 Engineer Regiment who support both the British Army and the Royal Air Force. Their key skills in offering ground support to the air components of the Armed Forces naturally compliment the work of the RAF.

The RAF Mountain Rescue Service based at Lossiemouth is deployed to about 25 incidents each year. A provisional service was formed whilst World War II pilots were training, due to the large number of crashes occurring when flying in areas of high ground with poor visibility. The RAF Mountain Rescue Service was formally established shortly after World War II and joined by the RAF Search and Rescue Service in 1986, continuing until the helicopter squadrons were disbanded and the Search and Rescue Service was assigned to the Bristow Group, a private organisation. The iconic yellow Sea King helicopters make up part of the interactive exhibitions at the **Morayvia Experience** (❶morayvia.org.uk) in Kinloss.

RAF Lossiemouth was established in 1939 as a training station, until it was taken over by Bomber Command. In the post-war years, it transferred to the Fleet Air Arm and operated once again as a training station, this time for RNAS Lossiemouth, also known as HMS Fulmar, until 1972 when the FAA service transferred to RNAS Culdrose in Cornwall, and the base was handed back to the RAF as a fast-jet facility.

RAF Lossiemouth continues to be an important presence in Moray. As well as the Mountain Rescue Service, four Typhoon squadrons and two Poseidon submarine-hunting squadrons fly out of the airbase, accompanied by the new E7 Wedgetail (Airborne Early Warning and Control Aircraft). Recent years have seen huge amounts of investment and the Poseidon Force building itself is bigger than Murrayfield, the home of Scottish Rugby.

The presence of the RAF at Lossiemouth and the Army at Kinloss are not just of importance to the nation's security but also to the economy and communities in Moray as they bring employment opportunities to the civilian population, skilled workers in the form of the partners of serving personnel, and pupils to bolster the school registers. The wonderful quality of life in Moray with the opportunity for outdoor pursuits, stunning surroundings and vibrant communities means that many military families choose to remain in Moray once their service has ended.

In the summer of 1940, the threat of German invasion was very real, and the Moray Coast was identified as an area which was vulnerable to enemy landing. A series of defence structures were constructed between Cullen Bay and Burghead Bay, and through Roseisle and Lossiemouth forests. On Burghead Bay, a line of concrete anti-tank pillars remain, interspersed by three small gun station pillboxes.

Burghead Bay was also the test site for an unusual military vehicle: the Valentine Tank. In anticipation of the D-Day landings, semi-aquatic tanks were trialled in the bay. Fitted with skirts, the tanks, (nick-named 'Donald Ducks') were launched from off-shore crafts and should have been able to propel themselves towards the beaches of Normandy, but during trials in the Moray Firth, they either sank or failed to propel in the rough seas. Due to the secret nature of the operation, the locations of only two sunken tanks are known: one in Findhorn Bay is a war grave, and the other is in Burghead Bay and can be dived using the co-ordinates N57 40.695, W3 39.651.

SAFETY AT SEA

With so many fishing communities along the Moray Coast, having a search and rescue (SAR) service is very important.

For over 150 years the Royal National Lifeboat Institution has served the community from Buckie. Today, the largest boat in the RNLI's fleet is on call in all weathers, ready to take on the worst sea conditions in long off-shore search and rescue missions. Although there are twenty volunteers at Buckie, only six crew members are required to operate the lifeboat. Fast, powerful, and capable of towing large vessels out of danger, it is also equipped with a smaller lifeboat to enable rescues in caves and shallow water.

HM Coastguard has a team of nineteen volunteers at Burghead providing a 24/7 maritime and coastal search and rescue service. The station operates from a unit by the harbour and has two jeeps which are equipped with ropes for rescuing trapped climbers, and some minimal equipment for water rescues. Although the dedicated staff are all volunteers, HM Coastguard comes under the auspices of the Department for Transport which funds all their equipment and facilities.

The Moray Inshore Rescue Organisation is a voluntary service based at Findhorn Boatyard and Marina which was established in 2005. Funded by community fundraising and charitable donations, the crew of MIRO use an inshore rescue boat to respond to incidents which happen within three miles of the coast on the stretch of the Moray Firth from Nairn to Burghead.

As the number of visitors to Moray increase, so do the number of call-outs which these services are required to attend. From rescuing dogs and walkers who have fallen down a cliff, to attending paddleboarders in difficulty and ships in distress, the highly trained team members who attend these missions are all volunteers. Rescues may also be attended by SAR helicopters which since 2013 have been provided by the private firm Bristow Search and Rescue. If you or anyone else require the services of any of these providers, please call 999 and ask for the Coastguard.

A TASTE OF MORAY
Wi' drink for my thrapple an' meat for my wame
John M Caie *The Puddock* 1934

The Moray Coast still provides employment for many fishing villages, with boats landing daily hauls of shellfish, cod, herring, mackerel, and haddock. Langoustine is a speciality of the Moray Firth as it is one of the few places around the UK where these creatures make their burrows in the mudflats.

Traditional livestock farming of cattle, sheep and pigs are raised on grass pastures; the rivers provide fresh salmon; and venison is reared on the Glenlivet Estate by Wild Farm.

Wild red deer can also be found in many local butchers – occasionally roe deer and sika are also available. Traditional game birds are plentiful in terms of partridge, grouse, and pheasant, as well as duck.

Game shooting opportunities are to be had on estates including Rannas near Buckie, where game stalking of deer is practiced as part of the estate management.

The traditional Scots diet was high in fat, which would have been very important to sustain a worker's body whilst they were fishing or farming, but the modern sedentary lifestyle doesn't require the same calorific burst. That doesn't mean you shouldn't indulge in tasty treats and one of the best ways to start your day is with a cup of tea and a **buttery**.

Fresh or toasted, this salty, fat-laden bakery item, (also known as a 'rowie'), is best described as a squashed croissant and can be found all across Moray and Aberdeenshire. Historically, the buttery was favoured by fishermen as its high fat and salt content ensured it was well preserved whilst they were at sea.

The Scots are notorious for having a sweet tooth, and the award-winning Fochabers Ice cream Parlour is drawing visitors from far and wide with 26 flavours which are home-made, every day, as well as a range of home bakes of indulgent specialities including apple crumble blondies.

For a grown-up treat, **Balvenie St. Dufftown** create award-wining luxury ice cream which is combined with fine single malt whiskies. **Stew 'N' Drews** in Hopeman, (and a new shop pending in Buckie), have created cask-strength whisky ice creams and sorbets, as well as an Elvis Juice ice cream in

Soup of the day

Cullen Skink is a culmination of the beautiful produce available locally, from both the land and the sea. This meal would have been made by the fishermen of days gone by using evaporated milk once their fresh supplies had expired or soured.

If the village you are staying in doesn't have its own fishmonger, there's a good chance it will be visited at least once a week by a mobile fresh fish van, stocked up from one of the fish markets along the coast - quite possibly at Buckie.

Get yourself a smoked haddock fillet, then pop down to the farm shop and pick up a few basic ingredients, (onions, potatoes, butter, and full-fat milk).

Soften roughly diced onions in the melted butter, then add the peeled, chopped potatoes, and milk - simmer. In a separate pan, poach the haddock in some of the milk. Once the fish has cooked, flake the tender meat from the skin, into your pan of potatoes - add your poaching milk to this too.

For a touch of luxury, finish with double cream.

Of course, it's much easier to pick up a tub of Whitehills Cullen Skink from the village shop - you will find their single-serving tubs in many locations.

If you want the real deal, head over to Cullen as the fishing village has given its name to the creamy smoked haddock soup. For seven years running, the World Cullen Skink Champions have been held here – most recently at the Cullen Bay Hotel. Competitors can enter *Traditional*, and *With a Twist* categories.

In 2020 both categories were won by Margaret Macrae at Kyle of Lochalsh. The west coast of Scotland is a bit far if you are just popping out for lunch, so you might like to try the Royal Oak in Cullen itself - they came a close second in the Championship (34 Castle Terrace ☎01542 842762 ⏻theroyaloakcullen.co.uk).

Wherever you dine, you won't be disappointed in this hearty soup of fragrant smoked fish.

collaboration with the Aberdeenshire punk brewery, Brew Dog. Their range includes non-alcoholic flavours the Edible Hulk, and Lovely Buttery – ice cream with butteries!

A WEE DRAM

Locally, much agriculture has been taken over to grow barley for the whisky industry, and in terms of classification, any whisky produced in Moray is considered 'Speyside'. Many of Moray's distilleries are to be found along the route of the River Spey, but there is a smattering of others across the region, including visitor-friendly distilleries Glen Moray in Elgin and Ben Romach in Forres. Moray has over 50 distilleries – the largest concentration of whisky distilleries in Scotland.

New in 2018, the vast Macallan Distillery has been designed with the visitor in mind and aims to stimulate all the senses with a fine dining experience.

The Cabrach Trust is currently working on a project to re-open an old distillery. With its take on heritage methods and tales of the illicit whisky trade, the distillery will operate as a social enterprise and all profits will be re-invested to the Cabrach Trust which aims to promote this remote part of Moray, located on the northern fringe of the Cairngorms National Park.

At distilleries across Moray, the iconic Chinese-style pagoda roofs of the malting kilns are now mostly decorative, as the demand on production requires that barley is malted to a distiller's specification at a large scale maltings before being transported to the distillery. Designed by architect Charles Doig in 1889, *Doig's Ventilator* is technically a cupola and was cleverly designed to draw the warm air up through the malting barley which lay on the kiln haircloth below. It replaced a more traditional oast house style conical ventilator and was extremely popular, with Doig installing it in 56 distilleries all over Scotland.

The Malt Whisky Trail (maltwhiskytrail.com) features seven working distilleries – Benromach, Cardhu, Glen Grant, Glen Moray, Glenfiddich, Strathisla and The Glenlivet – the fascinating Speyside Cooperage, and a self-guided museum housed in former distillery, the Dallas Dhu. Whisky can be either malt or grain, and Moray has the highest concentration of malt distilleries in the world. A single malt is made with malted barley and produced at one single distillery. It can be blended from many different whiskies produced by that one distillery but will remain a single malt.

Moray is well represented on the buzzing gin scene. Juniper grows wild in Scotland and is paired with other local botanicals to create unique flavour combinations. Let's start with Gordon Castle Gin, and Elgin's quasi-eponymous El:gin. Launched in 2016, El:gin combines traditional botanicals with local soft fruit and a touch of creamy oatiness, whilst managing to remain gluten-free. Gordon Castle Gin uses botanics grown in the walled garden of the castle's estate near Fochabers to create award-winning traditional and flavoured gins.

Gordon Castle also has a foot in the small batch brewery scene with a range of ciders, (produced from their own orchard), and a Scottish Pale Ale made from barley grown on the estate.

A visit to the Benromach Whisky Distillery will also give you the opportunity to get acquainted with their Red Door Gin.

Falling just outside the borders of Moray, but within the remit of Speyside, is Caorunn Gin. Made in Cromdale using local bog myrtle and rowan among their botanicals, you can take their tour at the Balmenach Distillery.

At the foot of Ben Rinnes, is the organic Glen Rinnes Distillery which makes gin and vodka in the brand "Eight Lands" – named for the eight counties which can been seen from the summit of Ben Rinnes on a fair day.

Keith's premium, small-batch distillery, Roehill Springs Gin is made on the family farm at Newtack outside Keith. Look out for their award-winning No. 5 gin, and their new blue colour-changing gin in the Speyside Whisky Shop in Aberlour.

Avva Gin is produced in Elgin by Moray Distillery Limited which is one of the smallest distilleries in the region. They produce gins, liqueurs, and a bourbon – book one of their tours and enjoy four different tastings as part of your experience. For more information about gin production in Scotland, please visit ⬛ginspiredscotland.com.

The oldest microbrewery in Moray is Spey Valley Brewery, established in Mulben (AB55 6YB) in 2007. Their humble brewery sits opposite a warehouse site owned by whisky giant Chivas, and although they can't offer you a tour, you can buy some of their lovely ales from the on-site shop.

Keith Brewery Ltd (aka Brewmeister) shares the premises with Spey Valley Brewery and claims to make the world's strongest beer – Snake Venom, coming in at 67.5%, should most definitely be consumed responsibly. A very popular drink in the Asian market, a bottle of Snake Venom is priced at £49.99.

Windswept (⬛windsweptbrewing.com) in Lossiemouth tapped into the craft brewery scene in 2013 and has been winning awards ever since. Drop into their Tap Room for a tour with the extremely knowledgeable Andrew and sample six of their tasty brews.

Whisky (and Gin) Distilleries with Visitor Experiences

Aberlour AB38 9PJ &01340 881249
☺aberlour.com
Ballindalloch AB37 9AA
&01807 500331
☺ballindallochdistillery.com
The Balvenie
Dufftown AB55 4BB &01340 822210
☺thebalvenie.com
Benriach Elgin IV30 8SJ
&01343 682888
☺benriachdistillery.com
Benromach* - *includes Red Door Gin*
Forres IV36 3EB &01309 675968
☺benromach.com
Cardhu*
Archiestown AB38 7RY
&01479 874635
☺discovering-distilleries.com
Cragganmore
Ballindalloch AB37 9AB
&01479 874715
(temporarily closed)
☺malts.com
Dallas Dhu Historic Distillery*
IV36 2RR &01309 676548
☺dallasdhu.com *(child friendly)*
GlenAllachie
Near Aberlour AB38 9LR
&01340 872547
☺theglenallachie.com
Glenfarclas
Near Ballindalloch AB37 9BD
&01807 500345
☺glenfarclas.com *(child friendly)*

Glenfiddich*
Near Dufftown AB55 4DH
&01340 820373
☺glenfiddich.com *(child friendly)*
The Glenlivet*
Near Tomintoul AB37 9DB
&01340 821 720
☺theglenlivet.com
Glen Grant*
Near Craigellachie AB38 7BS
&01340 832118
☺glengrant.com
Glen Moray*
Elgin IV30 1YE &01343 550900
☺glenmoray.com *(child friendly)*
The Macallan
Easter Elchies AB38 9RX
&01340 872280
☺themacallan.com
Moray - *Avva Gin*
Elgin IV30 6NB &07787 541561
☺avvascottishgin.co.uk
Strathisla*
Keith AB55 5BS &01542 783044
☺maltwhisydistilleries.com
Tomintoul AB37 9AQ
&01807 590 274
☺tomintoulwhisky.com
(temporarily closed)

*Malt Whisky Trail distilleries
Speyside Cooperage
Craigellachie AB38 9RS
&01340 871108
☺speysidecooperage.co.uk

MORAY AND MACBETH

Shakespeare's Macbeth is a murderous, treacherous man whose ambition to be king is fuelled by his wife's desire for power. Macbeth's reign of terror continues after he becomes king, killing more people out of paranoia, until civil war erupts, and Macbeth is overthrown – but just how much of this is true?

Born in 1000AD the real Macbeth was mormaer of Moray, but never Thane of Cawdor as he was hailed by the three witches.

We first meet Macbeth with his companion Banquo on a dark, wet night as they travel to tell King Duncan of their victory in battle. Three witches appear to the men, prophesising of Macbeth's destiny to be king of Scotland.

There are many stories of witchcraft in Moray, including one from the 10th century about three Forres witches who allegedly made King Duff seriously ill. The location of the Shakespearean encounter with the witches has been identified as Macbeth's Hillock near Brodie. You can book glamping accommodation nearby at ⬛macbethshillock.co.uk. The nearby castle at Brodie was constructed in the 16th century and is open to visitors.

After meeting the witches, Macbeth is welcomed to Forres by King Duncan at his castle. A castle did indeed exist in Forres during Macbeth's time, but King Duncan never lived there. The earthworks now form part of Castlehill Park.

On the edge of Forres, the huge carved Pictish obelisk that is Sueno's Stone would certainly have been known to Macbeth. The tallest piece of Pictish art in Scotland, it features a giant cross carved on one side, and scenes from a furious battle on the other.

Shakespeare had Macbeth murder King Duncan in his bed. In Macbeth's time, Spynie Palace was accessible by sea. It has been argued that this is where King Duncan landed his army before marching to Pitgaveny where Macbeth defeated him. After they met in battle, Duncan was killed, and his body taken to Elgin Castle. Only a ruin remains of the castle which stood on top of Lady Hill, commanding fabulous views over Elgin.

In both timelines, Macbeth becomes king of Scotland following Duncan's death. Shakespeare's nobleman Macduff encourages Malcolm (the son of King Duncan), to raise an army against the tyrant at Dunsinane, near Perth. A battle did take place here, with Macbeth defending his position against Northumbrian forces led by Earl Siward. The battle was neither won nor lost and Macbeth retained his life and title. In the Scottish play, Macduff challenges Macbeth during the battle at Dunsinane and returns victorious to Malcom with the traitor's severed head.

The real Macbeth was victorious in battle against Malcolm at Lumphanan in modern Aberdeenshire, in 1058, but died several days later from wounds received in the conflict.

Mormaer Macbeth and his wife Gruoch were both active Christians. Initially Macbeth was loyal to King Duncan of Scotland, but Duncan was power-hungry, and incompetent in combat. Duncan's attempt to get rid of Macbeth and bring Moray into his kingdom backfired when Macbeth defeated him on the battlefield.

Macbeth became king of Scotland at the age of 34, and for seventeen years life was peaceful and prosperous. Christianity was promoted and Macbeth enacted several good laws, one of which required officers of the court to defend women and children anywhere in the kingdom.

The final years of Macbeth's rule were turbulent as he fought off threats to the crown from the north and the south. He is buried on the island of Iona along with nearly 50 other great Scottish kings.

The people of Scotland, and Moray in particular, should be proud of Macbeth and recognise that he was a decent mormaer and king. The tragedy of Macbeth is that he is not generally recognised as such.

GETTING THERE & AROUND

Moray is well served by Inverness Airport in the west, and Aberdeen Airport in the east. Both airports have daily arrivals from many UK and international cities.

Inverness airport (🖱hial.co.uk) is located 8 miles outside of Inverness at Dalcross. Car hire is available at the airport and as the drink-drive limit in Scotland is lower than in England, just one drink could put you over the limit.

Stagecoach (🖱stagecoachbus.com) operate the Jetbus 10 service which runs all the way from Inverness to Aberdeen, (via Forres, Elgin and Huntly), 24/7, excluding Sundays. Alternatively catch the Stagecoach 11 bus to Inverness, before transferring to the eastbound train to Aberdeen, via Forres, Elgin, and Keith (🖱scotrail.com). Traveline Scotland has a handy website for working out travel routes (🖱travelinescotland.com).

Aberdeen Airport (🖱aberdeenairport.com) at Dyce, is served by the same connecting railway as Inverness Airport. A taxi or the X27 bus will take you to Dyce railway station for your ScotRail train to Moray. The X27 will also take you to into Aberdeen for the 10B bus service operated by Stagecoach, all the way to Elgin via Huntly, Keith and Fochabers. Alternatively, the 727 operated by Stagecoach North will take you an 8 minute journey to the Busburn stop on Inverurie Road, where you can catch the 10B enroute to Moray. Always check the timetables.

The Whisky Trail bus service is an enhanced version of the Stagecoach service number 36, which operates seven days a week from July to mid-August. Buses run hourly, connecting Elgin, Rothes, Aberlour, Craigellachie and Dufftown, with stops at a variety of distilleries along the way. Day-rider tickets for a group (up to 3 adults), are ideal for when no one wants to be the designated driver.

Moray Coast Day-rider tickets are available for the whole of the region. More information on ticket-types and zones can be found at 🖱stagecoach.com.

Arriving by car and your route will very much depend on you where you choose as a base for your trip. Book your first night in Forres, and you could find yourself travelling across the wilderness of the Dava Moor to your accommodation. Stay in Cullen and you will skirt past the grey, granite city of Aberdeen. Electric car charging points are available in most towns and can be found by checking ⬜zap-map.com.

Elgin is a main transport hub and is served by coaches and ScotRail trains between Inverness and Aberdeen. Trains also stop at Forres and Keith. Elgin serves as the station for local buses to most destinations in the area.

Dial M for Moray is Moray Council's award-winning accessible door-to-door bus service (public roads only) for those unable to use existing forms of transport or who do not have a regular scheduled bus service. This service is for everyone, regardless of age or ability, and operates over five areas: Buckie, Elgin, Forres, Keith, and Speyside. Hours of availability vary across the areas and transport must be booked by calling ☎0300 123 4565 (⬜moray.gov.uk).

It is worth noting that all buses accept only cash or National Concessionary Card as payment for services and there is no debit card payment facility available.

ACTIVE MORAY

With its combination of heathery moorland, stunning river walks and beautiful coastlines, Moray is a great place for many types of exercise.

Moray Ways (⬜morayways.org.uk/map) is an excellent resource that covers routes for walkers, cyclists, and horse riding. Zoom in to any location to find maps and directions or use the search facility on the homepage.

Forestry and Land Scotland (⬜forestryandland.gov.scot) produce handy maps of the forest areas with lots of information about local flora and fauna.

CYCLING

National Cycle Network Route 1 traverses the northern part of the county and for the majority of the way, it is an on-road route with a few, small, traffic-free sections. It eventually joins with Inverness in the west, and Aberdeen in the east.

Moray is excellent for mountain biking. The forests have plenty of trails for leisurely exploring as well as providing challenging sports trails.

Sanquhar Woodland Mountain Bike Trails – Forres

⬜forrescommunitywoodlands.org

One blue trail, and one red trail: perfect for a confidence-building introduction, and something for more experienced riders. For those who fancy practicing their drop-offs and jumps, there are also two training spaces at the orange section, Sanquhar Air Space.

Glenlivet Estate – Glenlivet

◉glenlivetestate.co.uk/outdoor-activities/mountain-biking

Discover biking for beginners, experienced cyclists, and free-riders at Glenlivet - their new orange trail is billed as, 'the best free-ride trail in Scotland'. Bike hire is available in summer, or by arrangement in winter.

Moray Monster Trails – Ordiequish (near Fochabers)

◉forestryandland.gov.scot/visit/moray-monster-trails

Ordiequish offers 17 miles of single track mountain bike trails for all abilities. Full information on routes and access is on their website.

Lecht – Tomintoul

◉lecht.co.uk/mountain-biking

A year-round resort, the Lecht opens its ski lifts to mountain bikers in the summer. Offering a red and a blue trail, both designed by Peter Laing, the Lecht's MTB trails offer fun, fast trails described as 'mountain cross' which means they are suitable for those who wouldn't venture on a traditional downhill course.

Bike hire

Bike Revolution Lossiemouth ☎01343 549571

Bikespokes Findhorn ☎07801 365710 ◉bikespokes.co.uk

Dufftown & District Community Association for adult ebikes, childrens mountain bikes, and recumbent trikes.

◉dufftowncommunity.co.uk/community-type/bikes

WALKING

The Dava Way (◉davaway.org.uk) is a 24 mile path, most of which follows the old Highland Railway route from Forres to Grantown in Strathspey. For the most part, the trail is firm underfoot and across open countryside. At times it can be wet and rough, especially through the railway cuttings, and there are some parts where you are required to walk on the road. Terrain varies from farmland to moorland, to woodland gorges and so the flora and fauna are also diverse – from shaggy highland cattle to fallow deer, and bright yellow broom, to delicate purple orchids.

On the central section between Dunphail and Dava is the Edinkillie Railway Viaduct. Known locally as the Divie Viaduct, the seven-arch viaduct was completed in 1863 and will carry you 170ft (52m) above the River Divie with fabulous views to either side. The highest point is the Dava Summit 1050ft (320m), and trains which would have arrived from the south required two engines to pull them up the incline. The Dava Way is also suitable for off-road cycling and the official website splits the route into three manageable sections, each with their own map, and comprehensive instructions for walking from either the north, or the south.

The **Speyside Way** (⬭speysideway.org) is one of four long distance routes in Scotland. It starts at Buckie and runs along the coast to the mouth of the River Spey at Spey Bay, then follows the path of the river to Aviemore – a journey of 65 miles. At Craigellachie a short 4 mile spur will take you to Dufftown; and from Ballindalloch, there is a 15 mile spur to Tomintoul. The name of the route refers more to the area than the river, so whilst some sections of the Speyside Way do follow the course of the Spey, cross over it, or just afford a glimpse, the route covers a diverse range of territories from the coast to the Cairngorms with great vistas along the way.

The official website can help with transport, accommodation, tours, and activities. There are two free camping areas: one at Fiddich Park, Craigellachie; and the other at Ballindalloch Station.

The **Moray Coast Trail** (⬭morayways.org.uk) is a breath-taking 50 mile walk from Cullen to Findhorn, which can then be extended along a section of cycle route to Forres to join up with the Dava Way. Discover the fishing towns and villages with their picturesque harbours. Navigate trails along the rugged cliffs, secluded coves and sandy beaches which provide a range of habitats for nesting seabirds and rare flowers. Enjoy wonderful views of the waters of the Moray Firth where you have the opportunity to see its most famous residents, the dolphins, as well as seals, minke whales, and even basking sharks. The walk has been split into ten sections to make it more manageable.

The **Moray Way** (⬭morayways.org.uk) combines the Dava Way, the Moray Coast Trail, and the Speyside Way into a challenging 100 mile walk. The website for the Moray Way also has notes and maps for 150 different routes all over the county, from a lunchtime walk around Elgin, to a wildlife wander around Loch na Bo near Lhanbryde. The website has excellent filter settings for distance and accessibility options.

Walk Highlands (⬭walkhighlands.co.uk) is another excellent resource for routes and maps across Moray, and nearly every town has its own website where you can download a PDF of local walks.

WATERSPORTS & COASTEERING

For paddleboarding, the beaches at Hopeman and Burghead offer calm conditions, whilst harbours like Findochty are safe and sheltered. For the more adventurous, you can enjoy the waves at Lossiemouth. Conditions at Lossiemouth are often favourable for surfing and windsurfing. Findhorn Estuary and Burghead Bay are popular with kite surfers. The Laich coastal area from Cummingston to Covesea offers a range of climbing and bouldering opportunities. A rocky outcrop near the Giant's Steps at Cullen is popular with rock climbers.

If you want to try water sports, climbing, or cycling adventures, Outfit Moray (below) host a huge range of activities.

Hire & Courses

JG SUP – Roseisle Country Park (📞07928 605168 🌐jgsup-rentals) offers stand-up paddleboard rental with a safety introduction and lessons.

New Wave – Lossiemouth East Beach (📞07818 238781 🌐newwavesurf.com) offers surfing lessons, as well as a hire service for surf boards and stand-up paddleboards.

Findhorn Water Sports – Findhorn Marina (📞01309 690099 🌐findhornwatersports.weebly.com) hires a variety of sailing boats to those with an RYA level 2 qualification, as well as sit-on-top single person kayaks, paddleboards, wetsuits and buoyancy aids.

Outfit Moray – Lossiemouth harbour (📞01343 549571 🌐outfitmoray.com) is based in Lossiemouth and offers a great many activities for friends and families. Equipment hire, such as paddleboards and canoes, is only available if you can prove you have the relevant qualifications. Alternatively, take part in one of their many organised outdoor adventures including climbing, abseiling, archery, bushcraft, coasteering, gorge swimming, hill walking, kayaking, mountain biking, paddleboarding, Tyrolean traverses, and weaseling.

Cullen Sea School – Cullen (📞01542 840830 🌐cullenseaschool.co.uk) offer lessons in kayaking and paddleboarding in the shelter of Cullen harbour. Try your hand at dinghy sailing in a one-to-one session or take a boat out by yourself if you can prove you're qualified.

FISHING

Grab yourself a cheap line and rod from a shop in nearly any of the seaside towns and try your hand at fishing from the end of the pier. If you are ready for the big-time, fishing charters are available from 2½ hours to 8 hours. There is usually a requirement of at least 4 people, and equipment is available for hire if you don't have your own.

Moray Firth Fishing Charters – Burghead Harbour (📞07808 514443 🌐morayfirthfishingcharters.co.uk) offers specialist opportunities for wreck and skate fishing, as well as half-day and full-day trips.

The River Spey is probably the most famous salmon river in the world, and the lower half is where the famous beats are to be found – Ballindalloch, Knockando, and Rothes to name a few. Salmon fishing is best from April to June, and the Spey is also one of the best sea trout rivers in the country.

Visiting anglers should contact the Aberlour Angling Association on Facebook, or the Fochabers Angling Association on ☎01343 821 029 for permits.

The River Lossie is fished for salmon and trout by rod and line from the mouth of the river up to Dallas. Originating in the hills above Dallas and flowing 31 miles (50km) to the sea at Lossiemouth, the lower 17.5 miles (28km) of the river is operated by Elgin & District Angling Association (The Angling Centre, Moss Street, Elgin ☎01343 547615). The Dallas Angling Association (☎01343 890420, ☎01343 890310) manages permits for the upper section.

Loch-based fishing for trout in the Lossie catchment area is available at Millbuies (☎01343 860234), Loch na Bo (☎01343 842214), Loch Romach, and Glenlatterach (☎01343 860234).

The Glen of Rothes Trout Fishery (☖glenofrothestroutfishery.co.uk) opened in 1994 and is a Troutmaster Competition fishery. It offers fly-casters the opportunity to fish on two trout lochs, set in a scenic glen. They can even offer rods, bait, tackle, and nets if you haven't brought your own.

HORSE RIDING

Moray Equestrian Access Group (☖meag2010.wordpress.com) has lots of great information about exploring Moray on horseback. Whilst they do organise riding events, access to these is restricted to members only. Non-members still have free access to 16 recommended trails on their website.

The Moray Ways website (☖morayways.org.uk) has a filter for selecting routes which are suitable for horse riding. For the beach rides, check the tide times at ☖tideschart.com.

Riding and Trekking Stables

Equus – Wards Crossroads, Roseisle, Elgin, IV30 5YP ☎01807 580210 ☖equusscotland.co.uk

Cranloch Riding Centre – Cranloch, Elgin, IV30 8QX ☎01343 842215 ☖cranlochridingcentre.co.uk

GOLF

Moray is home to a host of world-class golf courses. Enjoy the challenge of a links course and drive off the tee whilst looking out on the blue waters of the Moray Firth or play one of the inland courses with a backdrop of dramatic mountain scenery – just try to keep your eye on the ball.

Visit ☖morayspeysidegolf.com for information on all the courses in a handy PDF.

SKIING

The Lecht is a year-round resort, offering snow sports in winter, and mountain bike trails, quad bikes, and karting in summer. AB36 8YP ☎019755 651440 🖱lecht.co.uk

SWIMMING

Many of Moray's beaches are well known for their soft sandy bays and calm, clear waters which makes swimming in the sea a great holiday activity. Seven miles of unbroken sandy beach extend from Findhorn to Burghead. Hopeman and Lossiemouth each have a west beach and an east beach, and between the two locations, the beautiful cliff-backed bays of Covesea offer secluded swimming opportunities. The white sandy dunes of Lossiemouth's east beach gradually give way to shingle as it nears Spey Bay.

From Portgordon to Portknockie, the pleasant harbours and hythes offer safe sandy spits which are popular with families. Bow Fiddle Rock at Portknockie provides the opportunity to swim out to the bird colony on the iconic rock formation but you will need swim-shoes for the rocky cove.

Cullen boasts a long wide stretch of golden sand which features impressive rock formations, the Three Kings, and Whale's Mou. The curving bay is overlooked by cliffs and a large viaduct making it a very scenic spot for a swim.

There are no official lifeguard services but in the school, summer holidays there is a voluntary lifeguard service at Lossiemouth's East Beach.

Rip tides do occur and can be difficult to spot, but are sometimes identified by a channel of churning, choppy water on the sea's surface. If you do get caught in a rip tide don't try to swim against it. If you can stand, wade don't swim. If you can't stand, swim parallel to the shore until you are free of the rip, then head for shore.

Waterfalls make unusual and exciting places to swim. The water is much colder than the sea and the dark peaty waters can make it difficult to tell how deep the pools are. Randolph's Leap on the Logie Estate is a well-kept secret among local swimmers. Where once, a fleeing clansman sought to escape his foes by jumping the ravine across the River Findhorn, now wild swimmers can be seen taking the plunge into the cool waters of a still eddy below. For an easier option, head west along the river to the bridge at Relugas – from here you can walk a few hundred meters to find a quiet pool that is easy to access.

Set in a gorgeous woodland glen, Linn Falls at Aberlour are a short walk from Aberlour Distillery. Wade into the cool waters and relax as you watch the water tumbling down two sets of waterfalls.

TOUR MORAY

Glenlivet Hill Trek &01807 590 372 🖲glenlivethilltrek.com Full day Land Rover tours, and half day treks exploring historic Glenlivet and Speyside.

Moray Bespoke Tours &01309 641658 🖲moraybespoketours.co.uk Trips for 1-6 people, from 1.5 hours: wildlife watching, guided walks, salmon fishing and off-road safari excursions.

Scottish Marine Safari &07939 487518 🖲scottishmarinesafari.com Wildlife boat trips on a converted trawler from Buckie.

North 58° Sea Adventures &01309 690099 🖲north58.co.uk Wildlife and scenic tours from Lossiemouth and Findhorn.

Moray Firth Fishing Charters Burghead Harbour &07808 514443 🖲morayfirthfishingcharters.co.uk Fishing and wildlife tours available.

Wet Weather Activities

Ballindalloch Castle (page 112)
Brodie Castle (page 36)
Buckie and District Fishing Heritage Centre (page 128)
Elgin Museum (page 52)
Fochabers Folk Museum and Heritage Centre (page 99)
Keith & Dufftown Railway (pages 107 and 140)
Lossiemouth Fisheries and Community Museum (page 88)
Moray Motor Museum Elgin (page 54)
Morayvia Sci-Tech Experience Kinloss (page 48)
RAF & Fleet Air Arm Heritage Centre Lossiemouth (page 89)
Speyside Cooperage Craigellachie (page 111)

GARDENS OF MORAY

Warm air is brought to Moray on the Gulf Stream, and when this is combined with up to 18 hours of daylight in late spring and summer, the result is a long season of stunning gardens.

Glen Grant Distillery in Rothes (page 101) is not just for whisky lovers. The extensive gardens feature immaculate lawns, lily ponds, tall pines and beautiful borders, but the highlight is undoubtedly a wooden walkway which criss-crosses a dramatic gorge. Bright ferns and mosses cover the rockfaces of the gully, whilst below your feet the waters of the Back Burn tumble towards Glen Grant where they will be transformed into golden whisky. The gardens are open daily and there is no charge. Visitors are welcome to browse the distillery shop and enjoy very reasonably priced refreshments on the sunny patio. If you feel tempted, the tasting session is highly recommended – it comes with two very generous drams, and a friendly discussion with one of the distillery's knowledgeable team.

The public gardens at **Grant Park** in Forres (page 37) with their sunken gardens and award-winning floral animal sculptures are open year round and free to visit.

At **Logie Estate** (page 43) there is a trust box at the entrance to the gardens which sit below Logie House. Considerate planting and experimenting with the introduction of interesting and unusual plants has resulted in a garden which changes constantly. Woodland planting, a walled garden and large herbaceous borders showcase a wide range of plants which can thrive in these beneficial conditions. The garden at Logie is recognised as a Great British Garden.

Gordon Castle Walled Garden (page 99) is also listed as a Great British Garden. Lovingly restored in 2012, this is one of the oldest and largest kitchen gardens in Britain. The beds are arranged in terms of practicality, and everything that is grown is put to good use in either the café, gift shop items, or even delicately flavouring the Gordon Castle Gin. Design is at the heart of the garden. Busy beds of purple and white lavender surround the central fountain; towering, giant sweet peas are underplanted by bright marigolds, deep cosmos, ornamental thistles and more. Fruit trees are trained along the walls, and soft fruits including tasty strawberries flourish under the care of the expert team. Entry can be paid in advance online (🌐candidegardening.com), or by use of the trust box.

Brodie Castle Gardens (page 36) are free to visit every day (parking charges apply). Whilst it is known for its heritage daffodil collection, the east side of the turreted fairy-tale castle features sweet pea obelisks and deep flowerbeds. A large, ancient copper beech tree marks the entrance to a broad tree-lined avenue which invites visitors to enjoy a pleasant walk around the small loch.

Ballindalloch Castle Gardens (page 112) are open seasonally for a small fee and can be enjoyed separately to a castle tour. In early summer the gently curving flowerbeds of the walled garden are filled with delicate flowers, just waiting for the magnificent roses to burst into bloom. A separate rock garden offers splendid views of the romantic, ivy-clad castle with its towers, turrets and gargoyles. The castle is lived in by the Macpherson-Grant family, and the grounds are home to a prize-winning herd of Aberdeen Angus. A woodland walk through the castle grounds follows the banks of the rivers Spey and Avon.

Elgin Biblical Gardens (page 53) are free to visit and open daily from May to September. Every plant which is mentioned in the bible has been included in the colourful displays that form a narrative for well-known biblical stories.

In addition to these well-known gardens, Moray contains some hidden gems which are listed on Scotland's Gardens (🌐scotlandsgardens.org), a scheme that encourages people across Scotland to allow access to their gardens and raise money for hundreds of charities. Some of the bigger estate gardens are open from April to October, and other private gardens will just be open for one day or may require you to book in advance. The following gardens are open for several months – visit the Scotland's Gardens website to find out about more great spots which may only be open for a day.

Burgie Arboretum (Burgie Estate, near Forres IV36 2QU ☎01343 850231 🖱burgie.co.uk/burgie-arboretum) is an informal woodland garden which has an honesty box for charitable donations. From April to October visitors can explore themed sections including a rustic Japanese garden. Discover colourful rhododendrons, and plants from all over the globe. A small lake is home to a mating pair of swans and the gardens make for a lovely stroll. Burgie Estate is well known for hosting equestrian events and the stunning house is available as luxury holiday accommodation.

Haugh House (Roseisle IV30 5YE ☎01343 835790) has made a feature of a ruined 18th-century farmhouse located in a two-acre garden. Make an appointment to visit this secret country garden which is lovingly tended by Gwynne and David Hetherington. The green-fingered couple are as charming as their garden and will happily chat about the history of how the gardens at Haugh House have revealed themselves over the years. Enjoy a glorious riot of colour and texture in the flowerbeds and borders; walk down the avenue of mature trees to the old ruin; and explore a young woodland which follows a natural design and is a haven for wildlife.

Blackhills Gardens (Blackhills Estate near Elgin IV30 8QU ☎07780 680748 🖱blackhills.co.uk/gardens) is a private garden which specialises in rhododendrons. In this sheltered spot, over 360 varieties of this Tibetan plant come into flower in March, peaking in mid/late April, and continue to bloom right through to the beginning of June. Blackhills is home to one of the world's finest private collections of rhododendrons and visits are by appointment only.

FURTHER INFORMATION

Tourist information centres are located in Forres and at Elgin Library. Aberlour, Rothes, Cullen, and Tomintoul have seasonal services.

Visit Moray Speyside (🖱morayspeyside.com) has listings for restaurants and accommodation, as well as great ideas about where to go, and what to do when you get there.

For all you need to know about stargazing in Moray's Dark Skies Discovery Site, visit the website for Tomintoul and Glenlivet – Cairngorms Dark Sky Park (🖱cairngormsdarkskypark.org).

THE LAICH O' MORAY: INLAND LAICH

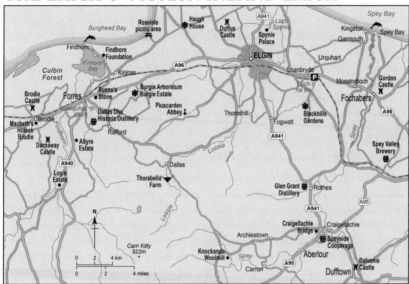

The rich, arable farmlands of the Laich have far-reaching views which are broken by dark patches of agricultural forestry. Here, you can explore the magnificent turreted castle at Brodie or wander through the woodland gorge alongside the rushing River Findhorn at Logie Steading. Find peace among the ancient ruins of a medieval abbey at Kinloss, or enjoy the Latin chants of the resident monks at Pluscarden Abbey.

The town of Forres has award-winning floral displays and hosts Highland Games in July. Moray's principal town Elgin features two museums and a majestic, ruined cathedral which was once hailed as the 'Lantern of the North'.

Forres, Brodie, and Elgin are served on the daily 10A service (from Inverness). Forres and Elgin are also connected by train on the Inverness to Aberdeen line. Forres, Kinloss, and Elgin can be reached on the 31A bus service – this service does not operate on Sundays.

BRODIE

If your journey to Moray takes you via Inverness, and you follow the A96 east, your first stop might be the hamlet of Brodie. The roadside verges are often covered in pretty, seasonal wildflowers, and the hamlet is home to **Brodie Countryfare**. A popular day out for coach trips and locals alike, Brodie Countryfare has grown over the years and features a bright family restaurant where you can snack on soup and a sandwich, or indulge in an award-winning afternoon tea. Before you make it as far as the restaurant, spend time shopping for unique Scottish gifts, hand-crafted home decor items, top-end designer clothing, or luxury foodie treats in the expansive warren of well selected goods.

Romantic, rose-tinted **Brodie Castle** (IV36 2TE ☎01309 641700 ⏣nts.org.uk/visit/places/brodie-castle) is just half a mile from the main A96 road, so if you are visiting by bus (10 or 10A from Forres or Elgin), it is a walkable distance.

The castle grounds are open even if the castle and tearoom are not, so enjoy a stroll around the woodland loch and admire the castle and its handsome turrets. At either side of the main entrance to the grounds, a pair of panels bearing the castle name, intricate metal work and the National

Explore a fairy tale castle set in beautiful grounds, and enjoy quality shopping at Brodie Countryfare.

Trust for Scotland logo welcome you to the grounds – the dark copper beech trees behind the panels, and flowerbeds of bright lupin spikes in the foreground invite you to travel down the long drive.

Just within the castle boundary is the **Rodney Stone**. At nearly 6ft (2m) high, this Pictish stone dates from the 8th century and was moved to its current location in the early 1800s. Set against the backdrop of an artisan fence of woven willow, the weather-worn sandstone contains engravings of a Pictish beast and sea creatures.

In springtime, the castle grounds are carpeted with over a hundred different varieties of daffodils, and throughout the year the fragrant flowerbeds which flank the castle walls are bursting with colours and textures. To the south-west of the castle, you can enjoy a walk down a broad tree-lined avenue and around the small lake. A country road separates the avenue from the lake, which is home to a variety of waterfowl including mute swans and mallards who are quite used to visitors.

The land was bestowed to the Brodies by Robert the Bruce over 700 years ago, and the castle has been extended over time – from a defensive tower to a magnificent turreted building, with ornate battlements and cannon drain spouts. If you have time, book a tour and explore the rooms and passageways with their beautiful antiques, interesting artefacts, and unusual plaster ceilings. There are many rooms which are open, over several floors and you should allow about an hour to be able to really enjoy discovering the interior charms of this castle which is as beautiful inside, as it is outside.

Macbeth's Hillock is a natural knoll which has long been associated with the site where Macbeth met the three witches who prophesise his rise and fall. Today, visitors to Moray have the opportunity to stay at a glamourous, eponymous campsite near Macbeth's Hillock (⏣macbethshillock.co.uk). The newly appointed glamping site has five mini lodges, which have been designed to resemble witches' huts. Each quirky accommodation sleeps four people and has its own picnic bench and firepit. The Hillock itself is fenced off from the glamping site as there are sheep grazing on it, but it is still accessible and interpretation boards bring the stories of Shakespeare's Macbeth, and the real Macbeth to life.

DARNAWAY CASTLE

The private residence to the Earls of Moray since 1563, Darnaway Castle (IV36 2ST) was rebuilt in the early 19th century and is only open to the public once a year on Doors Open Day (⎘doorsopendays.org.uk). The event usually occurs in late September and provides free entry to places not normally open to the public.

The crenelated mansion sits in beautiful parklands, surrounded by agricultural forestry and royal hunting forests. The largest-girth broadleaf tree in Scotland, a sessile oak known as the Darnaway Oak (aged over 750 years), is located in the forest. Visitors to Darnaway Castle can expect to see the stunning Great Hall c.1450, which now forms the south wing: the high vaulted ceiling of the Great Hall is clad entirely in wood and is the oldest of its kind in the UK.

FORRES

Forres Tourist Information Centre 20 Tolbooth Street ☎01309 672244 ⎘visitforres.scot App: VisitForres ⊙Mon-Fri 10am-3pm, Sat 10am-12.30pm

Forres is one of the most beautiful small towns in Scotland and is well known for winning the Scotland in Bloom festival on many occasions with its stunning floral displays in **Grant Park**. In 2019, the voluntary team who organise the planting, including their signature peacock sculpture, were awarded the Queen's Award for Voluntary Service which recognises the 30 years of work, which is emphasised by the town's motto, 'We love where we live'. The park also features sunken gardens which have been created from the ruins of Forres House which was destroyed by fire in 1970.

The leafy setting of Grant Park is where the **Forres Highland Games** have been taking place each July since 1928. At midday, in full Highland dress, the Forres and District Pipe Band parade up High Street heralding the day's events, after which there is an opening ceremony in the park. Traditional heavy sports compete alongside track and field events, cycling and road running. Pipers and Highland dancers also compete throughout the day, and spectators can enjoy hospitality, shopping, and fun at the visiting fairground.

Grant Park is backed by **Cluny Hill**, clad in a forest of deciduous oak and beech. At the top the hill stands the crenelated, octagonal **Nelson's Tower** which was established as a monument to the Lord's victory at Trafalgar by the people of Forres in 1805. A programme of forest maintenance in 2017 cleared much dead and diseased trees and cleared unchecked growth which had hidden the iconic tower. A pleasant woodland walk from Grant Park will take you up the hill to the monument. From the beginning of April to the end of September, between 2 and 4pm, you can climb the 100 steps of the spiral staircase to the top and enjoy a fine panorama. If the Tower is open, a red ensign (visible from the park), will be flying from the flagpole. The upper rooms of the Tower house exhibitions of local photographs, and Nelson memorabilia. Should the tower be closed, you can take a rest at a well-appointed picnic table from which you can see all the way to Findhorn and the Moray Firth.

Beautiful floral displays and stunning architecture make Forres a picturesque destination.

Cluny Hill has a dark history. In medieval times, local women who were found guilty of witchcraft were put in a barrel, through which spikes were driven. The barrels were then rolled down Cluny Hill, and where they stopped, they were set on fire. The site of one such burning is marked by a stone and a plaque in the low boundary wall of the police station. Witch burnings were sanctioned by the Scottish Witchcraft Act of 1563 and continued for over a century with over 4,000 people being tried for witchcraft related offences.

The middle of town is dominated by the tall, domed clock tower of the **Tolbooth**. An office for the collection of tax and the dispensing of justice has occupied the site since 1586, and the foundation stone to the building as it currently stands, was laid in 1838. Designed in a Scottish Baronial style, The Tolbooth houses an elegant Regency Courtroom and a Victorian Prison. Managed by Forres Heritage (forresheritage.co.uk), the Tolbooth is currently undergoing renovations with the hope of re-opening it to the public. It is very likely that there had been a tolbooth here long before the 16th century, but when the Wolf of Badenoch (page 14) travelled through Forres on his way to torch Elgin Cathedral in 1390, he also set fire to many of the buildings in Forres, destroying public records in the process.

Just to the west of the Tolbooth, is the **Mercat Cross**. Forres has had a market cross since the 12th century and the current gothic cross, built in 1844, is modelled on Edinburgh's Scott Monument.

The neo-gothic grandeur of **St Laurence Church** has a commanding presence over the high street. Constructed of pink granite in 1904, it stands on a raised grassy mound, with banks of bright flowerbeds enhancing the soft-coloured stonework. With its many spires the church has the aspect of a cathedral – the tallest spire is 120ft (36.5m) tall.

As with many of the larger towns in Moray, there are examples of fine Victorian architecture. The Falconer Museum (unfortunately no longer open), situated on the high street was built in 1851. It is named for the brothers Hugh and Alexander, the former of which was a contemporary of Darwin.

Other notable sons of the town include Sir Alexander Grant, 1st Baronet (1864-1937). A Scottish businessman and philanthropist, Grant developed the secret recipe for McVitie's digestive biscuits.

The Edinburgh-born song writer and folk musician Roy Williamson (1936-1990) died in Forres. A member of The Corries, he wrote *Flower of Scotland*, the unofficial Scottish national anthem sung at sporting events.

Forres is known for its green spaces and prize-winning floral displays: the main streets leading into the old town are lined with a variety of deciduous trees, colourful flowerbeds and multiple hanging baskets which delight the senses as you stroll through town.

At the west end of Forres is **Castlehill Park** and Thomson Memorial. The black wrought iron gates featuring silver thistles which mark the entrance to the park were designed by Alistair MacDonald, son of Lossiemouth-born Prime Minister Ramsay MacDonald.

The grassy mound that forms the basis for this park is all that remains of the 12th-century Forres Castle, which was once a substantial royal household and the seat of royal power in Moray. The size of the site belies the size of the castle, as the development of Forres has encroached upon the grounds once occupied by the royal residence.

Dedicated to Crimean War Assistant-Surgeon James Thomson, the memorial in the park was funded by Thomson's friend and colleague Sir James McGrigor. Thomson died of exhaustion when he volunteered to remain in the Crimea, attending to 700 seriously wounded Russian soldiers, saving 400 lives in the process. Thomson was born in Cromarty, but McGrigor was refused permission to erect the monument there and so he put it where it now stands, on land he owned himself.

The Burn of Mosset flows past Castlehill Park, and under the double-arched Castle Bridge which features crenelated turrets. In summer the bridge is adorned with colourful planters. On the north side of the bridge is the **Rose Garden** where the Mosset expands into a pond and the formal landscaping provides a pretty location for a picnic. Feeding the ducks has long been a fun family activity here.

Walk north on Inverene Road, following the route of the Mosset all the way to the white-painted **Benromach Distillery** (🌐benromach.com), taking care when crossing the busy A96 road.

Surprisingly, Benromach doesn't take its water from the Mosset, but from Chapleton Spring in the Romach Hills, southwest of Forres. The distillery was first opened in 1898 and has been under the ownership of the Urquhart family (owners of Gordon & MacPhail), since 1993. Benromach is the smallest working distillery in Speyside, and one of seven listed on the Malt Whisky Trail. It features the iconic pagodas of Doig's Ventilators and has the honour of having produced the first single malt whisky to be fully certified as organic by

Walk: Tolbooth to Sanquhar Loch 2 miles (3.2km)

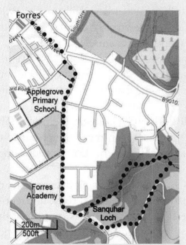

To help visitors explore the town and surrounding areas, Forres Foot Paths Trust (⌖forresfootpathstrust.org.uk) has established a network of paths which are signposted by yellow arrows on lamp posts and way-markers. There are twelve different routes available as PDFs with lots of information about points of interest. As well as the option to explore the town's highlights in under two miles, there are other walks that will stretch your legs for up to eleven miles, taking you out to local beauty spots.

Starting at the Tolbooth in the middle of Forres, a ten minute walk south-east of the town takes you to Sanquhar Loch, a haven for birds and wildlife.

A black Victorian-style signpost with gold lettering will direct you down Tolbooth Street. At the roundabout, cross straight over to Sanquhar Road and continue past handsome granite town houses with immaculate gardens on your left, and the tree-lined parks and school grounds on your right.

The end of the road is just beyond Forres Academy, and shortly after passing the school grounds you arrive at a small parking area for the loch. The paths around the loch are well used by local walkers and nature lovers, and an interpretation board shows the paths and illustrations of local wildlife.

The resident ducks and a pair of breeding swans are used to visitors and will swim towards any new pedestrian hoping for a treat. A short walk around the loch and over a wooden footbridge will take you back towards the beginning where picnic tables and benches provide an opportunity to relax and admire your surroundings.

A series of improvements is underway, (ending in 2023), which includes maintenance of the pathway, and tree management. The loch was created in 1900, and even though it is silting up, this process is actually encouraging biodiversity as plants encroach on the loch, providing new habitats for wildlife.

Look out for dippers dashing out from their nests behind the cascading waters of the dam.

the Soil Association. Pop in for a dram at their 5-star rated distillery, operating from a brand new visitor centre.

At just over 21ft (6.5m) tall, **Sueno's Stone** is the tallest, and most intricate Pictish stone in Scotland – standing next to it, one can really appreciate the size and detailed carving of the monument. Protected from the elements by a glass case since 1991, the sandstone pillar stands on the edge of town as you arrive from Kinloss and can be reached via the cycle bridge, or by car. Carved with detailed vine work on the sides, the west face shows a highly decorated Celtic cross, and the east contains four panels depicting a narrative of heroic battle scenes. Dated 850-950, the monument was found buried in 1726. The stone was initially named after the Danish king Swein Forkbeard, but the timeline suggests this may not be correct. An alternative history associates it with the killing of Dubh, king of Alba, in 966AD.

FORRES FOOT-TAPPER FESTIVAL
Since 2017, this real ale festival has showcased more than 20 breweries, from Scotland and beyond. Visitors to the three day event can also expect gins, tasty Cajun street food, and lots of live music.
Held at the Mosset Tavern, tickets are available on a daily or weekend basis. With the opportunity to sample over 80 real ales from Scottish craft brewers, and more than forty gins, you will probably need a weekend ticket! ⬤foottapper.co.uk

---

Food & Drink

The Mosset Gordon Street ☎01309 672981 ⬤mossettavern.com
A popular choice with locals, the Mosset occupies a spot by the rose Garden which makes summer dining a particularly pleasant experience. If you would rather sit inside, there is the choice of a casual bar meal, or main dining – either way, it is the same extensive menu showcasing local produce, traditional dishes and tasty alternatives including a pulled BBQ jackfruit burrito.

MacKenzie & Cruikshank West Road ☎01309 696940 ⬤mackenzie-cruikshank.com
On the western edge of Forres, this garden centre also houses a coffee shop. Famous for its scones (but also serving hot soup and tasty light lunches), The Potting Shed coffee shop is located at the end of a giftshop which is packed with beautiful items including quirky cards with Scots phrases, decorative homeware, clothing and jewellery.

Knockomie Grantown Road ☎01309 673146 ⬤knockomie.co.uk
This beautiful country house set in 4 acres of gardens on the southern outskirts of town is a stylish, 15-bedroom inn, with a restaurant which is open to the public. The menu is modern and constantly changing to reflect the seasonal availability of game and fish, as well as catering to vegetarians. Relax afterwards and sample a dram or two from their Malt Whisky Library.

DALLAS

The **Dallas Dhu Historic Distillery** (IV36 2RR ☎01309 676548 ⊕historicenvironment.scot) is closer to Forres than Dallas as it is less than two miles south of the former, on the narrow Mannachie Road. One of eight attractions on the Malt Whisky Trail, the distillery was last operational in 1983. The white-painted buildings feature the iconic Doig vent and even when the distillery museum is closed, the grounds are open year round so you can nosy around and have a look in the worm tubs where long copper coils snake around enormous water-filled vats. Walkers on the Dava Way can leave the route and pop in for a tour or just make use of the picnic tables – there is a large outdoor area that backs onto a section of flooded field which is full of insect and birdlife.

As there is no active whisky production it means there are no age restrictions, so it is suitable for youngsters. It also means you have access to areas which might otherwise be off limits in a working distillery. Tours are self-guided so visitors can take their time exploring different elements of the whisky making process and get up close to the stills and equipment which would be too hot or dangerous at any other distillery. After learning about the history of the Dallas Dhu, you also have the opportunity to have a wee dram of the popular Roderick Dhu whisky which the distillery was best known for producing.

The small village of Dallas is a further seven-and-a-half miles southeast of the distillery, in the flat fertile farmland of the Laich. Despite a population of about 200, it has a strong community spirit and each July, the Dallas Gala draws many visitors from the local area.

South-west of Dallas is a family-run farm called **Thorabella**, (IV36 2RZ ☎07753 383409 ⊕thorabellabuffalo.co.uk). The enterprising Lake family has developed from a self-sufficient smallholding with a few pigs, goats, ducks and chickens, to a 47-acre farm. Highland cows were added to the mix, as were rare-breed Gotland sheep. Keen to find a unique selling point, Thorabella has become home to a small herd of water buffalo. These big, black, friendly beasts form the main source of income for the farm, producing meat which is lean and tasty.

Visitors to the farm shop are likely to find buffalo pie and buffalo lasagne alongside staples such as steak, sausages, and burgers. If you have time, the Lake family would love to take you on a tour of their farm and give you the chance to meet some of their gorgeous animal friends.

LOGIE ESTATE

Built as a model farm in the 1920s, Logie Steading (IV36 2QN ☎01309 611378 🖰logie.co.uk) was bought by Sir Ronald Grant, and three generations of his family currently live on the estate. Just six miles south of Forres, Logie Steading is popular with locals, and its grounds are devoid of coach-loads of tourists.

Stunning river walks, gorgeous gardens, a popular café, and unique shops.

When you drive down the twisting roads to get there, you will understand why.

The long drive up to the steading is flanked by fields where you regularly see some of the Estate's prize-winning Longhorn Cattle (they really do have impressively long horns). Meat from the herd supplies the Farm & Garden Shop, and you can also buy wild venison from the Estate.

Re-imagined as a centre for creative business in 1991, the steading was transformed into a modern tearoom and workshops which included an art gallery. It proved to be popular with visitors and has expanded to incorporate the River Findhorn Heritage Centre and the excellent Farm & Garden Shop. A range of independent businesses including an antiques restoration workshop, a used-bookstore, a specialist whisky shop, and unique clothing and gift boutiques offer lots of excellent shopping. Logie Steading Gallery is filled with creative pieces by talented artists, and the walls of the coffee shop are also used to display canvases and prints which are for sale.

It's not just the delicious meals and tempting cakes at the Olive Tree Café which keep visitors coming back – the grounds of the estate include forest walks, and the formal gardens of Logie House which are open to the public – there is an honesty box if you would like to show your appreciation.

Logie House is a romantic 17th-century Baronial mansion, and the turreted, three-storey house is backed by a dark forest. Painted white, with stonework accented in grey, the house certainly makes its mark on the landscape. The beautiful gardens are included in *Britain's Finest* and frame the house with gentle landscaping. Carefully cultivated planting has resulted in a delightful garden that changes through the seasons, showcasing some interesting and unusual plants – many of which are for sale in the estate shop.

Logie Steading and Gardens are open year round, and in the summer months you can enjoy open-air theatre performances. With something for everyone, from Shakespeare to musicals and children's shows, these outdoor experiences are a big hit. Tickets are available from the Logie Steading Art Gallery and online – just bring a chair and wear something warm.

Logie Steading to Randolph's Leap 2miles (3.2km) 1 hour

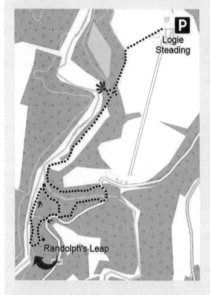

This popular walk has some narrow paths alongside steep drops so care should be taken, and dogs should be kept on a lead. Look out for red squirrels and blue jays in the trees.

From Logie Steading, access the children's play area via a wooden gate and head along the grassy path to a viewpoint above the river. From the viewpoint, there are a variety of walks: red arrows indicate a link to one of the newly developed Sluie Estate walks downstream from Logie; head west to follow the route of the river going upstream, and then follow the signpost marked Randolph's Leap via B9007 – there is also the option to head back to the steading from the sign.

The path follows the route of the River Findhorn to its junction with the River Divie, and then follows this smaller river until reaching the B9007. As you pass by a field you may see some of the Estate's friendly Longhorn cattle. Now you need to turn right on the road and cross the old stone bridge. Take care walking along this short distance of road until you spot an interpretation board and the entrance to Randolph's Leap on your right.

Access to continue the walk is through a wooden gate. As you head

Enjoy a network of walks by the River Findhorn as it tumbles through dramatic woodland gorges and waterfalls, and into dark swirling pools. Children love the play park, and the estate also offers exciting salmon fishing for those who are interested.

ALTYRE ESTATE

Altyre Estate (IV36 2SH ☎01309 672265 🖵altyre-estate.co.uk) is about seven miles south of Forres and has been home to the Cumming Clan since 1286 when Walter Comyn was made Lord of Badenoch. The estate is comprised of huge tranches of woodland, a grouse moor, and 2,000 acres of land used in arable farming and beef production. The River Findhorn runs through the estate, and part of the income of the estate is derived from hunting and fishing events hosted by the Laird.

The approach to the estate is an unmarked road which branches off the A940 in an easterly direction, into the woods. Almost immediately, it narrows downhill towards the river, look out for a Flood Stone on your left – there is another of these later in the walk and they indicate the height the river reached during the floods of 1829.

Randolph's Leap is in the narrowest part of the gorge. It can be accessed down a short muddy slope, and people do wild swim here, leaping from the rocks into a dark, peaty pool of still water. One of the greatest dangers associated with wild swimming is the shock of entering cold water, so do take care if you intend participating.

The story of Randolph's Leap is that of 14th century clan warfare. To the west of the River Findhorn, the land was owned by Thomas Randolph, Earl of Moray; to the east, by Alexander Comyn, (now Cummings). The two families had clashed, and Comyn's eldest son Alastair led an assault of 100-1,000 men against the Earl (sources vary as to the number of men assembled). The Earl's forces chased the intruders back. Alastair and four of his followers made it to the banks of the River Findhorn and jumped the chasm.

If you want to deviate from the official walk here, and head upstream, you might just come across Scotland's second tallest tree! Look for a small clearing to your right. Last measured in 2013, the Stika Spruce was recorded at 210ft (64m). It is next to a Douglas Fir which was measured at 197ft (60m), but it starts a few meters higher up the bank – the pair tower above the neighbouring trees.

Back on the main path and a little further on from Randolph's Leap you will find some rough steps descending to a viewing platform. Whilst it is not the best location for viewing Randolph's Leap, it does offer great views downstream, along the river.

Continue heading downstream and the path will turn right where the Divie and the Findhorn meet. You will find a second flood stone nearby.

The path will bring you back to the wooden gate. Retrace your steps along the road to Logie Estate and head up the drive to the Steading for some excellent retail therapy, followed by a refreshment at the Olive Tree Café.

to a single-track road, winding through beautiful deciduous forestry which soon gives way to tall pines. Go past the single-storey estate office building on your left and follow the road as it sweeps round to reveal a beautiful red wooden church with delicate, white-latticed windows, tucked in a little clearing. Funded in 1900 by Lady

Heritage, nature, and hidden gems reveal themselves at the Altyre Estate.

Gordon Cumming, this Victorian chapel with its simple wooden interior is used for private worship by the family and is also available for weddings. The deep red colour is associated with the Cummings and can be seen throughout the estate.

Nearby is Altyre House, a rambling two-storey house set behind a low hedge. Originally built c.1895 to accommodate the minister, the house was enlarged in 1931 when it became the Cumming family home.

Ahead, a plain of softly swaying grassland is topped by a stunning collection of Italianate farm steading buildings, their soft-ochre render accented by dark red woodwork. Dating from c.1834, and known collectively as Blairs Home Farm, this cluster of buildings fell into disrepair after lying dormant for decades. In 2015 a deal was agreed upon with Glasgow School of Art, and the buildings have been lovingly restored to create a truly inspiring world-class facility for Masters and PhD students. The picturesque tower and steadings now provide state of the art research labs and dedicated workspaces for the Innovation School where students investigate how research and design can have a positive impact on real-world situations.

Altyre Estate contains many tracks through woods and farmland which provide safe routes for walking and cycling. There is much to enjoy as you take in the charming lake bursting with irises, spend a while admiring the handsome herd of Aberdeen Angus cattle, or watch the pheasants strutting through the fields.

Among the historic sites to discover is Altyre Kirk. A well preserved ruin of a medieval Gothic church, it is illustrative of how the estate has been involved with the local community as along ago as 1220. The simple, rectangular-plan building is now roofless and contains three tombstones, one of which is an 1812 table tomb for Robert Cumming of Logie.

Hunting has been a popular pastime on the estate since the 13th century and there is evidence of a castle dating from this time. It is likely that the castle was still in use for some 200 years, but if you want to find it you will have to look hard for the remains. Southwest of the ruined 13th-century Altyre Chapel and overlooking the Altyre Burn is a regularised natural hillock, several meters high, with a flat oval summit capable of housing several large buildings. At the base of the hillock are traces of a ditch. The mound is heavily overgrown with trees and has a track winding around the slope to the summit, around which are possible traces of a rough unmortised wall.

Standing solitary in a field, guarded by a wooden fence, is the **Ogham Stone**. A tall slender slab of grey sandstone from the late 8th or 9th century, it was relocated to Altyre from Alves sometime in the 1800s. Worn and weathered, the faces now contain just traces of their decorative crosses and long inscriptions in the medieval ogham alphabet of the Picts.

Throughout the estate there are fascinating historical features including the splendid stables with their baronial turrets, an abandoned folly, and Blairs Loch with its handsome boathouse which was recently restored as part of a community project by the Friends of Blairs Loch (blairsloch.com). The Friends have also been busy constructing a bird-hide, re-purposing the old fisherman's bothy into a field study centre, and making the loch a special place for wildlife and the local community.

Altyre Estate Map points of interest

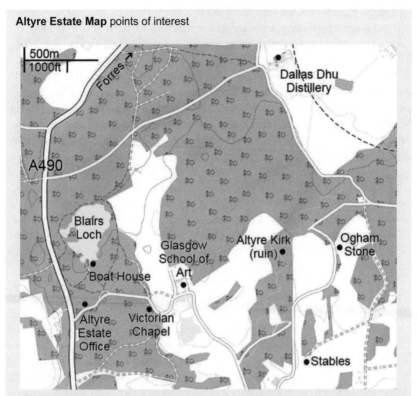

Altyre Estate is private land but due to the Scottish Outdoor Access Code you do not need to request permission to gain access to the trails, providing you are respectful and responsible.

Enjoy exploring the loch, farm, and woodland paths, keeping an eye out for cuckoos, kestrels and stonechats. Depending on your route you might even end up at the Dallas Dhu Distillery.

KINLOSS

The small village of Kinloss is closely associated with British military services. It was home to the Royal Air Force from 1939 until 2012 when the RAF standard was lowered for the last time, and control of the base was transferred to the 39 Engineer Regiment of the British Army.

During World War II, Kinloss operated as a training airfield. Post-war, Kinloss became home to the RAF's fleet of Nimrod aircraft which were used to monitor Russian ships and submarines in maritime patrols. RAF Search and Rescue, and Mountain Rescue services were also co-ordinated from the base.

The 39 Engineer Regiment compliments the history of Kinloss with about 800 personnel providing air support engineering to both the RAF and the Army. The airfield at Kinloss is maintained as a relief landing ground for nearby RAF Lossiemouth.

Morayvia Sci-Tech Aviation Museum (North Road ☎01309 691916 🖰morayvia.org.uk ⏰weekends 11am-5pm seasonal) was awarded Museum of the Year by Aviation Heritage UK in 2019. Carrying on the work started by the Nimrod Heritage Group, Morayvia has spectacular displays of machinery and equipment. If you spot someone wearing a flying suit, the chances are they have operated some of the aircraft that you can see and will be delighted to answer any of your questions.

Discover medieval abbey ruins and amazing modern aircraft at Kinloss.

In the first part of the exhibition, you might come face-to-face with Peter, a former Red Arrows pilot, who also knows about the ejector seat and tiny cockpits of fighter jets which are included this portion of the display.

The entire operations centre of the former Search and Rescue operation has been relocated to the museum. Helmets, uniforms, cartography, life-rafts and more: it's a fascinating insight into the important role that this service provided.

Outside, climb aboard the iconic Wessex and Sea King helicopters and imagine yourself as the pilot on a daring rescue mission. Explore the forward fuselage of a Nimrod and learn from a former crew member how they would track Russian submarines or locate people lost at sea. The interactive aerospace visitor centre has more than a dozen outdoor exhibitions including a Jaguar, a Vulcan, and an Antonov AN2.

The exhibition continues indoors with a staggering amount of machinery. There is a visceral smell of engine oil and engine enthusiasts can indulge their passion with another friendly, knowledgeable, jump-suited team member who is on-hand to discuss the technical aspects of the various pieces of equipment.

Morayvia took over the work started by the Nimrod Heritage Group which campaigned to save the last Nimrod from RAF Kinloss from destruction. Re-named *The Duke of Edinburgh*, it can be seen at the end of the runway from the B3011 road to Findhorn. Morayvia is a fabulous, immersive experience brought to life by the opportunity to talk to the crew and ground-staff who operated and maintained the aircraft.

In contrast to the hi-tech attraction of Morayvia, are the beautiful ruins of **Kinloss Abbey**. Founded by King David in 1150, Kinloss Abbey was one of the largest and wealthiest religious houses in Scotland, which received royal visitors including Mary Queen of Scots in 1562. The Scottish Reformation, signalling the end of Catholic control, had been passed in 1560, and over the decades the monks were not replaced, naturally dying out. In 1643, the abbey was purchased by Alexander Brodie of Lethen who sold most of the stone to Cromwell's army for use in the construction of their citadel at Inverness in 1652.

The ruins of Kinloss Abbey include the remains of the south transept, cloister walls, and beautiful arches, and a tomb and vaulting in the interior of the sacristy. The local cemetery has been developed in the grounds of the abbey, and the presence of the RAF is reflected in lines of Commonwealth war graves.

Cyclists in Kinloss will find a convenient fixing station located by the Spar shop at the junction of the road leading to Findhorn where they can fix flat tyres and tighten loose bolts.

Nearby is the Abbey Inn (Findhorn Road, ℃01309 690475 ⓕabbeyinnkinloss) serving hearty, home-made pies, and tasty curries. If you fancy cooking up something at home, visit the Woodside Farm Shop (℃01309 690258) at the east end of Kinloss to stock up on homegrown produce and create your own farm-to-fork experience.

PLUSCARDEN ABBEY

Set in the peaceful glen of the Black Burn, surrounded by beech trees, and backed by the dark Douglas firs and Scots pines of Torrieston Forest, medieval Pluscarden Abbey was established as a monastery in 1230 by King Alexander II. The abbey suffered major damage, twice, in its early history: the armies of Edward I of England (Hammer of the Scots), ravaged Pluscarden in

Pause to listen to the haunting, Gregorian choral chants of the Pluscarden monks.

1303, and then the Wolf of Badenoch set fire to it in 1390 on his way to destroy the cathedral at Elgin. The boundary walls date from the early 13th century and enclose fruit and vegetable gardens. Four Irish yew trees in the walled garden may date from the original layout.

When Scotland converted to Protestantism in 1560, the monasteries were not dissolved as they were under Henry VIII in England but were allowed to die out with their monks and such was the fate of Pluscarden in 1595.

For the next 350 years the Catholic Priory passed through the control of lay-priors, but was mostly abandoned, save for a little private worship and some use as a burial place by local families. The roofs fell in, woodwork rotted, and the church and cloisters filled with rubble until 1943 when an Anglican Benedictine community were given the priory and its land. After much hard work, the monks were able to take up residence five years later, and in 1974 the status of Abbey was bestowed upon the monastery.

Today, Pluscarden is the only medieval monastery in Britain inhabited by monks and being used for its original purpose: a training place for novices, and a place of worship, work, and reflection. Visitors to Pluscarden are invited to park their cars and approach on foot, sustaining the tranquillity of life at the Abbey (onsite parking is available for those less able). Visitors can explore several sections of the abbey buildings and grounds, as well as attend Mass or sung prayers between 4.30am and 8.30pm. The ethereal vocals of Gregorian chants, sung in the original Latin resonate throughout the superb acoustics of the sandstone Abbey. Spiritual retreats are also available, giving the opportunity to participate in aspects of monastic life including prayer and work.

Pluscarden was built to impress. The great Rose window in the north gable is 16ft in diameter and would have greeted medieval visitors arriving on the old Pilgrim Road. Only a few fragments of the medieval stained glass windows survive and are preserved in a case. The modern windows are bright and modern decorative jewels, most of which have been created using the *dalle de verre* technique – literally, glass paving slabs. The technique produces thicker glass than traditional methods, resulting in rich, saturated colours, which flood the interior of the building when illuminated.

The Rose window and north transept were created by Scottish stained glass artist Sadie McLellan, between 1964-67.

A depiction of St Andrew in leaded glass is attributed to Crear McCartney, but many of the windows have been created by the monks themselves in their own stained glass workshop and are stunning pieces of artisanship in their own right.

The monks subsidise their income with a giftshop where you can purchase CDs of their sublime choral chants, and seasonal honey from their own bees.

ELGIN

Elgin Tourist Information Centre: Elgin Library, Cooper Park &01343 562608 ☉ Mon-Fri 10am-8pm, Sat 10am-4pm

Medieval Elgin was a cathedral city with access to the Moray Firth: a sea loch that extended to Spynie Palace and offered safe anchorage to fishing boats and merchant vessels. **Elgin Castle** was a royal residence to four early Scottish monarchs: built on the grounds of a former defensive castle, some believe King Duncan died there of his wounds inflicted by Macbeth.

In the 19th century, Elgin was flush with commerce and industry. The building of Spynie Canal had helped reclaim much of the low-lying lands, transforming them into rich agricultural grounds. Later, construction of the railway line to Lossiemouth was key in the prosperity of Elgin, as was the later addition of the town on the Inverness to Aberdeen line, putting Elgin on an economic crossroads, dealing in crops, distilling, and fabrics. By 1882, Elgin was re-designed with neo-classical architecture, and boasted a Head Post Office, banks, hotels, a newspaper, and many offices associated with a busy, important centre of commerce.

From Castle to Cathedral to Cashmere – discover the heritage and history of Moray's principal town.

Today, the town itself has a more relaxed air despite retaining much importance as the centre for local governance. The remains of Elgin Castle are to be found at the top of **Lady Hill**, from where George Gordon, the 5th Duke of Gordon (an agricultural reformer), presides atop his 80ft column. Looking east from here, you can easily see the dome and tower of St Giles Church. Between Lady Hill and St Giles was the medieval Royal burgh of Elgin.

Elgin has some handsome sandstone buildings in Georgian and Victorian architectural styles, and two of these are a result of sons of Elgin who amassed considerable wealth whilst working abroad.

In the west end, an impressive hospital with Doric columns and a beautiful dome was built by the bequest of Dr Alexander Gray who had made his fortune with the East India Company, for the 'sick and poor of Murray' [sic].

East of the town centre, General Andrew Anderson, who had also attributed his wealth to the East India Company, established Anderson's Institute to provide welfare for the elderly poor, and education for orphans. Anderson himself had a harsh existence from childhood, sleeping in the ruins of the cathedral and relying on the generosity of others.

In middle of Elgin high street, is the **Plainstones.** Locally referred to as 'the Plainstaines,' it is an area which formally established for market traders in 1787. At the centre of the Plainstones stands St Giles Church. With its classical portico of six Doric columns, and a tower rising 112ft, the church has echoes of Greek architecture both inside, and out. Inside St Giles, is one of the finest organs in the north of Scotland.

Leading off from the high street you will find lots of narrow lanes, wynds and closes –remnants of the layout of the town's medieval history. Just off the high street, Thunderton House is one of the oldest buildings in Elgin. Now a shadow of its former self, it dates back to the 16th century when it was a popular residence for visiting royalty, including Bonnie Prince Charlie on his way to battle at Culloden. Legend tells that the landlady at the time kept the prince's bedsheets and was eventually buried in them.

On South Street, the whisky merchant Gordon & MacPhail occupies a particularly fine building which is full of golden treasure for those who enjoy a dram, or something a bit more unusual.

In 2016, the historic centre of Elgin became home to three sculptures which were commissioned to showcase the town's history – and are not without controversy.

At the west end of the town, *The Wolf of Badenoch* a sculpture of Alexander Stewart is stylistically framed by a gothic arch of the cathedral, as he raises his sword angrily towards the Duke of Gordon. The two would never have met: in 1390, The Wolf infamously set fire to Elgin cathedral, and the duke was born some 220 years later.

On the Plainstones, the colourful *Dandylion* represents the traders. His lion's head is a nod to the lion rampant on Elgin's Muckle Cross – the local name for the large market cross, symbolic of a town's right to hold fairs and markets. Elgin's Muckle Cross consists of a hexagonal balcony which sits 12ft high on the Plainstones: in the centre of this cross, a tall shaft is surmounted by the Scottish Lion. Although the current Muckle Cross dates from the 1880, the lion belongs to the original cross which was erected in 1630. Fine attire boasts of Elgin's prosperity, whilst a boutonniere of a dandelion echoes the days of the Feeing Market when people looking for employment would advertise their availability on market days by wearing a dandelion flower on their clothing. The fishy tail of the merlion is a homage to the fisherwives and other traders who would bring their wares to market.

Least controversial is *Elgin's Town Drummer* at the east end of the Plainstones: a statue of William Edwards, the last person to hold the position of town drummer, who died in 1822. William held the position for 60 years –his job included waking up the town's folk at 4am to go and work in the tanneries and mills.

Elgin Museum (1 High Street &01343 543675 []elginmuseum.org.uk) is away from the pedestrianised Plainstones, and at the far east end of the high street. Opened in 1843, it is the oldest independent museum in Scotland. The Italianate style architecture was chosen to stand out in its Victorian setting and to show off the collections. The museum proudly holds Recognition status for its internationally renowned collection of fossils which includes the Elgin Reptiles. Older than the dinosaurs, these fossils include the large herbivore *Elginia mirabilis*, a life-size replica of which can be found at the museum. The Main Gallery, People and Place, tells the story of Moray's last 1,000 years, while elsewhere you will find archaeological treasures including examples of Treasure Trove, a fine display of Pictish and Early Medieval carving and the last remaining Speyside currach (coracle). Upstairs, changing displays and art exhibitions regularly showcase new and fascinating collections to the public.

Upon arrival, you will experience a friendly welcome from a volunteer who will give you a brief introduction to the beautiful A-listed building and the exhibits. Most of the displays are on the ground floor but it has not been possible to install a lift. It is recommended that you book a time slot on the museum's website for your visit – entry is free so please consider donating generously.

Outside of the museum stands the Little Cross, marking the boundary between secular Elgin and the religious Chanonry. A cross has been on this site since 1402. The sundial and top of the column are facsimiles of the original 1733 section which is now housed in the museum.

From the museum, make your way to the majestic ruins of medieval **Elgin Cathedral** (King Street ✆01343 547171 🎧historicenvironment.scot 🕐1 Nov to 31 Mar, daily 10am to 4pm, booking is essential). The foundation for 'The Lantern of the North' was laid in 1224, but then fell victim to a fire in 1270. It was rebuilt, and greatly enlarged – then in 1390, The Wolf of Badenoch in his battle with the Bishop of Moray torched the cathedral, (and much of Elgin), reputedly declaring, 'I have set fire to the Lantern of the North!'. The cathedral was repaired, and another incendiary attack followed in 1402. Repaired once more, Elgin Cathedral continued to be used until 1560 when its services were transferred to St Giles Church, and the building steadily fell into decay.

Today the cathedral is a fascinating tourist attraction, full of history. The octagonal chapterhouse with its vaulted ceiling has been beautifully preserved; the west front is comprised of the stunning architecture of a processional entrance flanked by two towers which have been repaired and restored, and the fragmented remains of the rose window are a reminder of how ornate the building once was. Elgin Cathedral contains more medieval stone memorials than any other Scottish cathedral, and tombs of bishops and knights are to be found in the choir. Two miles north of Elgin, Spynie Palace was the home of the Bishops of Moray for over 500 years.

In summer, the cathedral comes to life as actors tell the stories of the incendiary Wolf of Badenoch, John Shanks – a cobbler and early custodian of Elgin Cathedral – and the essential role of a medieval blacksmith in the daily activities of cathedral.

Near the cathedral, and through a handsome black iron gate topped with a pair of white doves are the peaceful **Biblical Gardens** (King Street 🎧biblicalgardenelgin.co.uk 🕐May to Sep, 10am-7.30pm). Set out in a Celtic Cross formation, this community horticultural project grows plants mentioned in the Bible and uses statues to tell well-known Biblical stories. The garden contains formal planting mixed with more natural areas of planting and makes a lovely place to enjoy a picnic. A beautiful rainbow of bedding plants welcomes you; clematis wind their way up a steel frame replica of the cathedral, and the changing fragrances as you move throughout the garden are a sensational delight.

The River Lossie meanders slowly past Elgin, looping out to the suburb of Bishopmill. It then skirts past Cooper Park before coming back down towards the cathedral, gently sweeping past Johnstons of Elgin, and eventually heading out to sea at Lossiemouth. It has been known to burst its banks (there have been about 20 floods since 1750, and a quarter of these were between 1997 and 2014), causing extensive damage to the surrounding area, and railway services to be suspended. Completion of the Elgin Flood Protection Scheme in 2016 has had a positive effect in the immediate area.

Luxury fabrics and fashions have long been synonymous with **Johnstons of Elgin**, (New Mill ✆01343 544088 ⊕johnstonsofelgin.com). A Scottish heritage industry, the Elgin Mill has sat on the banks of the River Lossie since 1797. Now established for over 220 years, the business may have had its early roots in tobacco and linen, but it soon declared itself as a leader in the wool industry. The firm started producing Estate Tweeds – and then in 1850 a bale of cashmere was purchased, arriving on one of the first trains from London to Elgin. Johnstons pioneered the weaving of Cashmere and Vicuna in Scotland. They were awarded a medal at The Great Exhibition of 1851, and continued exhibiting, and winning awards in excellence which led to their product being exported across the globe. Fine textiles are still produced at the Elgin Mill and the firm now graces the catwalk at London Fashion Week. Tourists are welcome to discover the story of Johnstons at The Cashmere Visitor Centre, where the waters of the River Lossie are still key in cleaning the fibres used in the production of luxury goods. Beautiful garments and home furnishings made with the finest fabrics are available in the on-site store, where you can also purchase locally produced desirable items, and relax in the Weavers Restaurant for a light lunch.

Housed in a converted grain mill, part of which dates back to the era of the cathedral, the **Moray Motor Museum** (Bridge Street ✆01343 544933 ⊕moraymotormuseum.org ⊙seasonal), pays homage to the glamour days of the motorcar. The vintage vehicles in this private collection are still in use, and regularly take part in rallies, races, and even films. If the magnificent Rolls Royce Phantom I is out on loan, there won't be a gap in the showroom as it will be replaced with an equally spectacular car from the private workshop. The light and airy building is adorned with classic signage relating to the automobile industry, and each vehicle has its own remarkable story to tell.

Mark on reception knows the collection inside-out and can tell you fascinating facts. Direct your gaze to a 1904 Speedwell with gorgeous racing-green paintwork and shiny brass fittings - it's the only known two-cylinder Speedwell to exist. The brass headlamp was powered by acetylene, created by dropping a pill of calcium carbide into a water reservoir. A sky-blue Daimler from 1910 was the star of BBC spy drama 'Ashenden' – with five pedals for operating the vehicle, it proved to be too big a challenge for actor Joss Ackland to drive!

Race-cars such as the 1957 silvery-grey Tojeiro Bristol are displayed with all their racing heritage, and there are several videos to enjoy. From the sleek E-Type Jag to the sporty Lagonda V12, cult classic microcars, and vintage motorbikes, the Moray Motor Museum has an exciting collection of full size vehicles, as well as cabinets exhibiting mint-condition miniatures. The private collection is a labour of love, and this is a great opportunity to get up close to some beautifully restored classic cars. Free parking is available just opposite the museum, and adult entry is priced at £6, which includes a free tea or coffee in a nearby coffee shop.

SPYNIE PALACE

Moray was one of the most important dioceses of the Roman Catholic Church in medieval Scotland, yet despite this, the early bishops did not have a fixed seat.

Birnie Kirk, built in 1104 was the first cathedral of Moray and is one of the oldest churches in Scotland to be in continuous use. The Kirk of Kinneddar which was cathedral from 1187 to 1208, and all that remains of it is the old kirkyard near RAF Lossiemouth. Spynie Kirk became the third seat of the bishops of Moray until Elgin Cathedral was established in 1224. The church was in use until 1735 when a new one was constructed some three-and-a-half miles away using many of the stones from the original building. The old graveyard is still located near Spynie Palace and is the final resting place of former British Prime Minister Ramsay MacDonald.

Such an important diocese required an impressive residence for its bishops, and for nearly 500 years, the fortified buildings at Spynie were the home of the bishops. The first castle was a 12th-century wooden structure, with stone buildings not appearing until the following century. The term 'palace' wasn't used until 1524.

Successive bishops developed the castle in the form of a quadrangle, with towers at each of its corners, one of these towers being built by Bishop David Stewart. At seven stories tall, David's Tower is the largest, by volume, of all medieval Scottish towers, and dominates the site. Inside, the tower is rather empty, but climb the spiral staircase for rewarding views across the Laich o' Moray including Loch Spynie – imagine how this looked to the bishops living here when the loch stretched all the way to the sea.

The last Catholic bishop to reside at Spynie died in 1573, and other than a brief spell when it belonged to Alexander Lindsay, 1st Lord of Spynie, it was occupied by Protestant bishops who continued to live at the palace until 1689 after which it fell into decay. This period in history was troubled times for Scotland, with civil war and threat of invasion by Spanish supporters of Mary Queen of Scots, and much was done to boost the fortifications of the castle.

Open to visitors from April 1 to September 30, Spynie Palace is in the care of Historic Scotland (historicenvironment.scot) and tickets should be booked in advance online to guarantee entry. A brown tourist sign opposite the access road on the A491 directs you to the dedicated car park. Alternatively, ask the driver of the 33 bus service from Elgin to Lossiemouth to drop you off en route, and walk the half-mile to the palace grounds.

LOCH SPYNIE

The RSPB reserve at Loch Spynie is a haven for wildlife. A huge medieval sea loch which served as the port for nearby Elgin, Spynie was drained in the 1700s by landowners to create the surrounding farmland. A canal was created, and water was pumped from the loch using power generated by windmills. In 1808, Thomas Telford was tasked with extending the canal which now runs seven miles to Lossiemouth.

The largest freshwater reed bed in Scotland, Loch Spynie is surround by deciduous wet woodlands, fen meadow and Scots pines. Regular visitors to the special habitat include herons, mute swans, grebes, and greylag geese. A hide has been set up with a view of the nesting platform on the loch which is often used by terns. The hide contains posters with images to help identify many of the other feathered creatures – perhaps you will be lucky enough to see a marsh harrier or kingfisher.

Red squirrels make their home in the trees around the lock and can be seen helping themselves to nuts from the feeding stations, which also attract many birds including woodpeckers.

Elusive otters, pine martens and owls can all be seen at Loch Spynie but even when the wildlife is quiet, the loch and short trails around it provide a perfect opportunity to relax in beautiful surroundings.

It is worth noting that the loch is not accessible from Spynie Palace. Access from Elgin is via the old B9103 Pitgaveny Road to Lossiemouth. At the crossroads for Spynie Churchyard and Calcots, carry on straight ahead to the single-track road. After a mile-and-a-half where the road ahead bends to the right, a farm track leads off to the left – this should be sign-posted Loch Spynie/Scarffbanks Farm. Follow the farm track, at the end of which there is parking for six cars.

LOCH NA BO

This little-known beauty spot just south of Lhanbryde provides a beautiful woodland circuit around a man-made loch. The surrounding woods are a mixture of pines and deciduous trees providing habitats for red squirrels, woodpeckers, and Daubenton's bats which forage for flies just above the water.

The main black route is three miles and can be short-cut along the grey routes. This is private land, and access is allowed by the Scottish Outdoor Access Code. Please be respectful of the privacy of Loch na Bo House, which is available as luxury, self-catering holiday accommodation from £3350 per week (⏻georgegoldsmith.com ☎0131 476500). Boat-based trout fishing is available by per permit (page 30).

There is a small parking area accessible form the B9103, but it is much easier to park at Threaplands Café & Garden Centre (IV30 8LN ☎01343 619870 ⏻threaplands.co.uk) where there is ample room for cars, and an excellent eatery and shop. After your walk, relax in their bright, airy café and enjoy generous portions of hot meals and amazing cakes. More than just a garden centre, Threaplands also stocks beautiful gifts, stylish homeware, and an excellent range of locally produced food and alcohol.

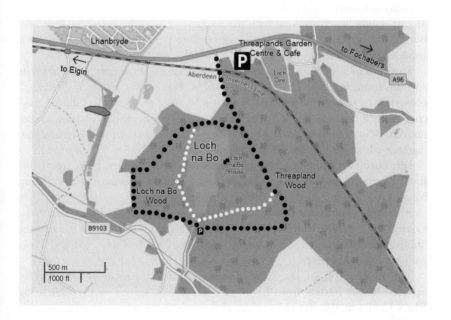

THE LAICH O' MORAY: COASTAL LAICH

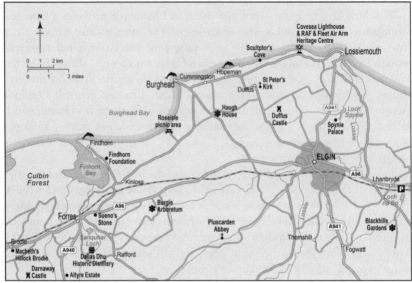

The coastal Laich features pretty fishing villages each with their own fascinating history. From Findhorn to Burghead, you can walk on seven miles of soft, sandy beach studded with the remains of wartime defences. Between Burghead and Lossiemouth there are pockets of picturesque beaches and secluded coves to explore.

Stretches of agricultural forestry and sandstone cliffs are enjoyed by wildlife and adventurers alike. In the west, Culbin Forest is a carefully managed ecosystem of sustainable pine trees which is home to a variety of wildlife. Criss-crossed by a network of trails, the forest is ideal for exploring by bicycle and on foot. Between the forest and the sea is an RSPB reserve of mudflats and salt marshes which provide important habitats for wading birds and waterfowl.

Kite surfers are often to be seen riding waves on the broad estuary of the River Findhorn, and all along the coast you will find opportunities to try your hand at fun activities such as sailing and paddleboarding.

Although you can drive, walk, or cycle between the villages along the Moray Coastal Trail, getting to them by bus is less straight forward. Elgin is a central hub for transport, and it serves Findhorn on a circular bus route (31 and 31D) with Kinloss and Forres.

The mid-section of Burghead, Cummingston, Hopeman and Duffus is serviced by the 32 bus from Elgin. Lossiemouth is served by the 33A from Elgin. Findhorn also has an excellent cycle-path all the way to Forres.

Culbin Forest Hill 99 Walk 3½ miles easy

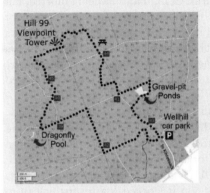

Below Culbin Forest lie the remains of a ruined 17th-century farm estate and croft cottages, buried under the shifting sands of the beach. Crofters would gather marram grass to thatch their cottages and fuel their fires, but without the grass there was little to keep the sand dunes in place. In 1694 a mighty storm whipped up the loose dunes and covered the community under a series of sand drifts.

It wasn't until 1850 that pines were planted to try and stabilise the environment, but it took a century of hard work – growing new grass and laying cut branches to trap the shifting sands – before there was a well-established forest at Culbin.

Stretching for more than 8½ miles west from Findhorn, Culbin Forest is full of paths which are ideal for exploring on bike or on foot. Wellhill car park (IV36 2TG) is £2 per day, and there are toilets here as well as an information board. Culbin is a large forest riddled with tracks, and major junctions have numbered posts to help you find your way. Maps of the forest should be available at the car park and online at ⏻forestryandland.gov.scot/visit/Culbin.

Hill 99 is waymarked by black arrows. The circular route begins at the Wellhill car park (ignore the path to the left as it is the return route) and winds through the pines on well-surfaced paths to an attractive area called Gravel Pit Ponds, a popular spot for birdwatching with a couple of well-placed benches. From here you will cross shingle ridges and lichen beds to gently climb Hill 99, Culbin's highest sand dune at 99ft (30m).

Climb the steps of the wooden tower for a superb view over the pines, taking in the salt marshes and sand flats of the RSPB reserve. A handy indicator shows which hills you can see both across the Moray Firth and behind you in the Cairngorms.

Descend the tower and take the path past the trig point, winding through the trees to junction 45, then head straight on to junction 40. From here, follow the narrow path to your right through mossy glades and emerge at Dragonfly pool which teems with wildlife in summer.

Turn left along a wide straight track. A right turn will take you towards junction 42 where you turn left. Follow the woodland track until a signed right turn directs you onto a narrower path which will eventually lead to the car park.

Culbin is full of wildlife and history. The Otter Pool is a favourite drinking spot with locals. Remnants of the salmon fishing industry and WWII anti-glider defences can be seen at the shoreline, where wading birds feed.

Culbin is a working forest so there may be felling operations in progress when you visit - please adhere to any safety signs and diversions in place.

FINDHORN

The houses in the historic fishing village of Findhorn are all numbered, but there are no street names, and you will find that this is the case with many of the traditional fisher towns in Moray. Luckily, this pretty village is not such a big place so when you are looking for The Kimberley Inn at 94 Findhorn, you shouldn't have too much trouble finding it. At low tide, the Findhorn estuary is a favourite fishing ground for ospreys, and The Kimberley is well positioned to provide an excellent spectator spot.

The proximity of the village to the Findhorn Foundation (The Park, Findhorn IV36 3TZ ⓘ findhorn.org) has been pivotal in the way that the former fishing village has developed into a creative, artistic hub. The Findhorn Foundation is internationally respected for its environmental practises. Located about a mile from Findhorn on the B9011, it is a tranquil retreat which attracts artisans and crafts folk. The Phoenix Shop is stocked with everything from healing crystals and books on new age practices, to organic produce grown on their own estate and elsewhere. A Visitor Guide is on sale at the shop and will help you explore the peaceful compound. Within the grounds of The Park you might see some unusual, round, wooden eco-houses – these dwellings have been made from re-purposed 9,000 litre whisky marrying vats. Workshops are available in a variety of disciplines from weaving to well-being, and there are often public performances by well-known comedians and musicians at the Universal Hall.

Try some fun water sports or take a wildlife boat tour at this pretty seaside retreat.

Historically, Findhorn has been an important fishing port since the 17th century. It was briefly served by a railway branch line from 1860 to 1880, and 19th century underground Icehouses are testimony to the success experienced by the local fishing trade at the time. The **Findhorn Heritage Centre** and **Icehouse** (ⓘ findhorn-heritage.co.uk) are two separate premises which contain fascinating exhibitions telling the tales of fishing throughout the years. The grass-covered mound of the Icehouse hides four red-brick vaults where ice would be stored in winter, ready for packing fish for transport during the salmon fishing season. Inside the cool chambers, exhibitions show scenes from a fisherman's bothy, harvesting ice, and preparing the fish for shipping. An intricate model shows how the staked nets would be set out in the sandy bay of the Moray Firth – you can see the stumpy remains of the wooden stakes at low tide on the beach at Burghead.

Across the road from the Icehouse, in a black wooden building, the **Findhorn Heritage Centre** has information about how the sea and sands have changed the landscape, and who has lived in the surrounding area from early human settlers to local wildlife.

The fortune of Findhorn and its inhabitants have long been governed by geography and weather. The original settlement of Findhorn was located one mile west along the coast, but was lost to the sands and tides. The prosperity of the harbour was hampered by the shallow bay silting up thus denying access to larger fishing vessels.

Modern Findhorn is very much a pleasure harbour. A pleasant stroll along the waterfront is accompanied by the chiming chandlery of small sailing boats docked at the sandstone piers. The Captain's Table towards the far end of the esplanade is a popular spot for drinks and meals with lots of outdoor seating.

Get your sea-legs on and climb aboard the bright orange rib, which is docked by The Captain's Table and operated by North 58° Sea Adventures (page 32). The North 58° team can take on you a 20 minute adventure to discover the beautiful village of Findhorn from the sea, and hopefully encounter some of the local seal population along the way. If you have more time, you can enjoy a two hour cruise which (with a little bit of luck) will also give you the chance to have an exhilarating encounter with some of the resident dolphins, as the experienced staff take you along the beautiful Moray Firth Coast and share their local knowledge about the area and its watery wildlife.

The Findhorn Foundation

Now an internationally renowned organisation, with recognition from the United Nations, the Findhorn Foundation has very modest roots.

In the early 1960s, Peter and Eileen Caddy were living at Findhorn Bay Caravan Park with their three young sons, and their friend Dorothy MacLean whom they had met through a spiritualist friend. Surviving on unemployment benefits, Peter decided to improve his family's situation by growing vegetables in the barren sandy soil – with huge success. Caddy attributed his success to their spiritual practices and a community began to form around his family and MacLean.

In 1967, Eileen published a book of guidance. The small community which was committed to 'inner listening', and 'co-creation with the Intelligence of Nature', gained new followers. A meditation sanctuary and community centre were built. The Findhorn Foundation was formally registered as a Scottish charity in 1972. By the end of the 80s there were about 300 members, and it had purchased the caravan park where it had its roots.

A logical step in the harmonious development of the community was the Ecovillage Project which was initiated in the 80s. The Findhorn community organised a conference in 1995 with other ecovillages, and from this, the Global Ecovillage Network was established – its role is concerned with developing strategies for sustainable communities for the 21st century.

The Ecovillage at Findhorn is used as a teaching resource by universities and school groups from all over the world, and in 1997 the Findhorn Foundation was recognised as a Non-Governmental Organisation by the UN for its work promoting sustainable development.

At the mouth of the River Findhorn, sandbanks curl around the mouth of the estuary, creating the illusion that it is possible to walk all the way across the bay to the vast expanse of pine forest on the far side of the river. The tall dark pine trees of Culbin Forest stand on top of pale, creamy dunes, holding the shifting sands in place and they form a huge area of coastal forest which stretches beyond the border of Moray, to the Highland town of Nairn.

The estuary is too wide, deep, and dangerous to be passable on foot, even at low tide. The easiest way to get to Culbin Forest from Findhorn is by water taxi – another service provided by the friendly team at North 58°.

The old harbour is a great place for a spot of crabbing or just for a relaxing stroll. Away from the waterfront, the Findhorn Pottery studio is where you will find unique hand-crafted pieces. Inspired by the sea, Lynne makes pieces which can be functional or decorative – but they are always beautiful.

At the Bakehouse you can sit down to enjoy a generous slice of cake and a coffee, before stocking up on delicious organic produce, and perhaps find that perfect memento from their selection of local arts and crafts.

The beaches at Findhorn are beautiful. The west beach is best suited to water sports as the dinghies and sailboats navigate out of the safety of the estuary into the bay where they can catch the breeze.

The beautiful soft sands of the sheltered east bay stretch for seven miles to the village of Burghead. Away from the pleasure boats, the east beach is great for a swim, and seals from the colony at Culbin can be seen bobbing about in the water. A row of new beach huts at the foot of the dunes adds a splash of colour, and the sunsets are spectacular.

Parking is available for the east beach by following Dunes Road just after you pass the Findhorn Foundation. West beach parking for cars, along with new facilities for motorhomes (IV36 3YE ⬭findhornparking.com) can be found near the marina at the far end of the village.

ROSEISLE

Roseisle is a rich farming region, separated from the sea by an excellent beach and a tall pine forest full of fabulous trails for exploring.

Notable local, Ethelreda Baxter (nee Adam), was the daughter of a Roseisle farmer. She fell in love with William, son of the Baxters founders George and Margaret, and went on to help create the world famous luxury food firm. Ethel was instrumental in managing the factory and devising new, delicious recipes.

The College of Roseisle is a small collection of houses on a crossroads, and the location for the stunning secret gardens of Haugh House which are set around an 18th century ruined farmhouse (page 34). From here, head west towards Kinloss and you will pass the Roseisle Distillery – considerable expansion since 2010 has transformed the maltings into the largest distillery ever built at a cost of £40 million. Owned by Diageo, the high-tech whisky production facility is controlled by just ten staff.

Roseisle's star attraction is the pine forest and soft white sands of the Country Park (IV36 2UB ⬤forestryandland.gov.scot/visit/Roseisle). Better known as Roseisle Picnic Area, this is a firm favourite with locals. Parking is charged at £2 per day and although it is not easily

Walk through sweet-smelling pines, and relax on a soft sandy beach at Roseisle picnic area.

accessible using public transport, the woodland trails lead five miles from Findhorn in the west, and just two miles to Burghead in the east and are perfect for a walk or cycle.

Picnic tables are dotted throughout the forest near the parking area, and purpose-built barbecues are available to help reduce the risk of forest fires. If self-catering is not your style or should you feel the need to have a barista coffee, G&M Whyte are on site with their Sausage and Burger Bar serving up gourmet hot food including venison burgers and halloumi wraps. The picnic area has a fun adventure park for children, and toilet facilities are open from April until the end of October.

The forest of tall pines is full of wide flattish trails which are suitable for walking, cycling and horse riding. Visit the official website to download a map featuring three short walking trails and discover an old icehouse and a fisherman's bothy from the days when salmon used to be fished with staked nets in the bay. The woods are home to roe deer, red squirrels, and a variety of birdlife. A hide on the west trail gives you a chance to watch small woodland creatures at a feeding station.

Down on the beach, oystercatchers scuttle at the shoreline whilst grey seals occasionally bob about in the bay. Concrete pillboxes and a long line of anti-tank blocks which were part of WWII defences are an iconic part of the shoreline. Slowly being consumed by the shifting sands these unusual features make great focal points for photography.

The gently sloping beach is safe for families and if you fancy trying something new, paddleboards can be hired from JG SUP (📞07928 605168 ⓕjgsup-rentals) who have a van full of equipment in the picnic area. The friendly team supply buoyancy aids and a safety briefing to help you feel confident about having fun on the crystal clear water at Roseisle.

BURGHEAD

Come again, come again ye Burghead men
Tae the Broch where you'll aye belong
To the Druid's Well the Clavie's smell
And the oystercatcher's song

Gordon Menzies, *Burghead Sands*

Steeped in ancient tradition and Pictish history, the peninsular fishing village of Burghead is flanked by rocky outcrops to the east, and a beautiful soft sandy beach to the west. Dolphins and seals are regular visitors in the surrounding waters, whilst the pine forest provides tranquil trails for walkers and cyclists to explore.

The village of Burghead is often referred to as 'The Broch' and people indigenous to the village are called 'Brochers'. In 1750, Burghead was a fishing hamlet which occupied a small part of a peninsula on the Moray coast, and home to a man called Alexander Stephen who had come from a farming family in Lossiemouth to establish a ship building yard in the fishing community. Stephen took on his nephew William as an apprentice, and in 1793 William went on to establish a branch of the business in Aberdeen where he persuaded his uncle to join him. The Burghead branch of the business continued building small coasting vessels for local customers and was managed by one of Alexander's children as Alexander Stephen & Son until 1826. The Aberdeen branch of the business went through some difficult periods, but eventually grew in strength and size, passing through six generations of ship builders who moved the company from Aberdeen to Arbroath, then Dundee and on towards the Clyde where it finally ceased trading in 1982 – but not before the Scottish comedian Billy Connolly had served his time as an apprentice there.

Explore the history of Scotland's largest Pictish fort at Burghead Visitor Centre.

The 19th century saw the greatest growth in sea fishing on the east coast of Scotland, and it was in 1805 that Sir Archibald Dunbar sold the village of Burghead and the surrounding land to William Young, Thomas Sellar, John Brander, Joseph King, George Fortreath, William Grant (Earl of Seafield), and the Duke of Gordon – who set about creating the village you see today. This enterprising group laid out a new village on the grid system, naming some of the new streets after themselves. They instructed the renowned Scottish engineer Thomas Telford to build a new harbour, coastguard station, and granary buildings in 1807. With its new harbour, Burghead became a busy port, and the granary buildings would have been used to store grain, potatoes, timber

Shopping, eating & drinking: **1** Drop into The Gather'n Café, Aberlour for a spot of lunch, and pick up some tartan thrums from 3 Bags Wool to craft your own souvenir.

2 Enjoy a tour at the Windswept Brewery, Lossiemouth, and finish off the day with a wood-fired pizza and a tasting flight of locally made ales.

History and heritage: 1 The majestic ruins of 'The Lantern of the North,' Elgin Cathedral. **2** The tallest Pictish stone in Scotland is Sueno's Stone, Forres. **3** Pyramids of barrels at the Speyside Cooperage, Craigellachie. **4** Take a trip to Keith from Dufftown heritage railway station. **5** One of four stones decorated with Pictish art at Inveravon Church. Ballindalloch.

History and heritage: 1 Heather priests were trained at the remote secret seminary of Scalan, Glenlivet. **2** Knockando Woolmill uses historic machinery to create exclusive small batch yarns and fabrics. **3** Johnstons of Elgin has been producing the finest woollen and cashmere clothing and textiles since 1797. **4** Book a tour of iconic Strathisla Distillery in Keith, home of Chivas.

Events: 1 A member of the Clavie Crew throws fuel on the fire at Burghead's ancient new year celebration, The Burning of The Clavie.

2 The massed pipes and drums lead a day of musical and sporting competitions at Aberlour and Strathspey Highland Games.

Festivals: 1 Keith Country Show is a fun two-day event featuring massed pipe bands, Highland dancing, vintage vehicles, sports and livestock competitions, and trade stands.
2 The Spirit of Speyside Whisky Festival opens the doors of some of the world's most famous distilleries. Live music, talks, tastings, tours and more, take place over six days.

Castles: 1 Rose-tinted and turreted, Brodie Castle is every bit the fairy tale castle. Tour the historic rooms, then explore beautiful gardens and woodland walks.

2 The impressive ruins of Auchindoun Castle sit on top of a hill, south of Dufftown. Enjoy panoramic views and discover the dark history of this dramatic castle.

1

Gardens: 1 Gordon Castle has one of the largest walled gardens in Britain. Relax among the flowers and sample the produce at the award-winning café.

2 The colourful creatures at Grant Park are part of the fabulous floral displays which keep the town of Forres winning horticultural awards year on year.

2

© SUNITA LINCOLN

© GEOFF LOWNDES

Sacred places: 1 The Baxters window at Gordon Chapel, Fochabers. **2** Mortlach Kirk, Dufftown features a Pictish stone in the graveyard. **3** Immerse yourself in the sound of Gregorian chanting by the resident monks at medieval Pluscarden Abbey, near Elgin.

and coal, as well as fish. Some of the granary buildings have since been converted into flats. William Young eventually bought out his partners to become the sole self-styled laird of Burghead.

The modern, charming fishing village of Burghead sits on a high headland, which commands views across the Moray Firth and to the hills and mountains of Caithness and Sutherland. The land rises gradually from sandy plains to a rocky sandstone precipice and has long been an important site – under the grassy mounds at the headland lie the remains of the largest historic fortress in Scotland. Between the 4th and 6th centuries AD, the Picts built a wooden fort at the top of the headland and protected it with a series of landward facing ramparts – the site was three times larger than any similar centre of power at the time and was occupied for 500 years.

The ramparts of the Pictish settlement would have occupied the area which now lies between Young Street and Bath Street. During the construction of the new village, most of the ramparts were destroyed and levelled out, with the rubble being taken away to fill areas around the new harbour, or for use in the construction of new homes.

Up to 30 stones which were decorated with highly stylised carvings of a bull were taken from the Pictish fort, and of these only six remain. It is thought that the stones would have adorned the fort and as the design on all stones is particular to the village, it has become known as the **Burghead Bull**. It was common practice in the 19th century that antiquities would be distributed among acquaintances of the finder, and this is what William Young did. Fortunately, he also sent one to the Society of Antiquaries in London which finally made its way to the British Museum. A second bull is at the National Museum of Scotland in Edinburgh, two are in the Elgin Museum, and two are on display in the **Burghead Visitor Centre** which is housed in the iconic round coastguard lookout station at the top of the headland. A modern replica of the Burghead Bull has been carved into a six-foot sandstone block which stands at the entry to the village on the road from Elgin.

The Burghead Visitor Centre (☏01343 835518 ⊓burghead.com ◷noon-4pm, daily, April-September) offers spectacular 360° views. From the look-out station on top of the former coastguard station, you can see the neighbouring fishing village of Hopeman in the east. Turn widdershins (anti-clockwise) and look across the Moray Firth to Caithness where the conical peak of Morven is easily identifiable. In the summer months you may well see a cruise ship sailing past, having travelled down the Cromarty Firth and made berth at Invergordon. You may also see an oil rig being pulled by tug-boat – the bay of the Cromarty Firth is used as a parking lot for massive rigs which can weigh up to a thousand tons each.

The Black Isle, a peninsula on the west side of the Firth, just north of Inverness forms the far side of the channel into which the Moray Firth flows. South-east of the Firth you might be able to make out the fishing village of Findhorn: from here you can walk across the seven miles of sandy bay all the way to Burghead. Your panorama is completed as your gaze travels across the extent of the village, past the peak of Clarkly Hill, and Maltings and back to Hopeman.

As well as great views, the Visitor Centre takes a look at the history of the village from 400AD to the present day. Imagine yourself in the Pictish fort – possibly trying to fight off marauding Vikings who captured the important seaport of Torridon (as Burghead was known) in the 9th century. The Vikings ruled Moray from the fort until they were defeated by the Scots in 1010. Discover the hard-working men and women of the herring boom: in 1834 the busy village of Burghead was important enough to have a regular steamboat service operating to Glasgow.

Of the old Pictish ramparts, only partial elements remain. On one of these grassy elements stands a blackened stone chimney: this is the **Doorie Cairn**, and it forms part of an ancient ritual called The Burning of the Clavie, which is unique to Burghead.

During the construction of the modern village in 1809, there was a shortage of water, but a local man recalled that there had been a well within the enclosure of the lower fort, and correctly identified its location. Today, access to the **Burghead Well** is via a locked gate, on the lane at the top of King Street. The key can be obtained from the Visitor Centre or from the Bothy Bistro on Grant Street – the Bistro has an excellent reputation for serving fresh seafood dishes in a casual dining environment.

Open the gate to the walled compound of the well, and you will enter an unusual space. Steep grassy banks sweep down either side of a flight of twenty stone steps which lead into the darkness of the well. A square chamber has been cut into the bare rock, surrounded on all sides by a 3ft (0.9m) ledge. The tank was 4ft (1.3m) deep and fed by a natural spring.

When the well was reclaimed in the 1800s, the chamber required clearing out and among the many objects recovered was another carving of the Burghead Bull, and part of a Pictish stone cross. Builders used gunpowder to deepen the tank and increase its capacity: at the same time, they re-cut the access steps, and covered the chamber with a vaulted stone roof which had a ventilation hole. The excavations led to the realisation that the flow of water to the well was insufficient to support the need of Burghead and it was abandoned once again.

In antiquarian and archaeological circles, the theory of the three-age system (Stone Age, Iron Age, and Bronze Age) was only really developed in the period 1816 to 1825, and although the Burghead Well was initially classified as Roman no-one really knows who built it or why. There is no other well like it in Scotland. Certainly, the inhabitants of the fort would have required a water source, although this one is on quite a grand scale. Perhaps it was also used as a baptismal font: the Picts were converted to Christianity and there are local

The Burning of The Clavie

On 11 January each year, the residents of Burghead celebrate the New Year according to the old Julian calendar. The only exception to this is if the date falls on a Sunday, in which case the festival is celebrated on the preceding Saturday.

On the day of the celebrations, the Clavie King and his crew of twenty-or-so local men set about putting together the Clavie: a half barrel is mounted on a wooden stake, using the same ship-builder's nail as in previous years, and hammering it in with a large stone; supports are added around the base and the barrel is coated with tar. Around the village, supplies of wood and flammable liquids are stored safely for later when the Clavie is carried throughout the old village.

Thousands of people flock to Burghead every year to witness the burning of The Clavie, but only men from the village whose forefathers have carried the Clavie before them are entitled to be part of the Clavie Crew.

Celebrations begin at 6pm on the Old Manse Dyke on Granary Street as the Clavie King brings burning peats from a local house to light the Clavie. The barrel contains five gallons of creosote, and it is stacked with timber stakes – within no time at all it is a fiery, burning beacon. The Clavie King calls to the crowd *hip-hip!* and he is met with a resounding *hooray!* Twice more the call is made, before the burning barrel is lowered onto the shoulders of the first member of the crew to carry it on its journey.

For over 45 minutes this flaming totem is borne through the streets of Burghead. Stops are made to hand out burned-out stakes to the local publicans and various houses – the charred remains of a piece of the Clavie will bring good luck for the rest of the year. New timber is added, and more tar is poured into the burning barrel, feeding the flames.

The festival culminates as the Clavie is carried to its final stop at the top of the Doorie Hill and carefully positioned in the ceremonial Doorie Cairn. More timber is added and then fuel is thrown on to the fire. The hillside is engulfed with flames and the delighted crowd cheer on the crew to throw more buckets of flammable liquids at the Clavie.

On a dry night with just enough wind, the smoke is lifted high above the village and the Clavie burns brightly.

Towards the end of the burning, the crew help distribute red-hot stakes to eager recipients – some of these pieces will be sent around the world to ensure that Brochers who no longer live in the village still get their share of good luck for the coming year. Once the fire on the Doorie Hill has been safely extinguished the crowds depart from the Doorie Hill to continue their New Year celebrations with friends and family.

references to the 7th-century missionary St Aethan. A second well attributed to St Aethan is located on the outskirts of Burghead, along the Moray Coast Trail towards Cummingston, but there is a site closer to the Burghead Well with greater significance than this.

At the top of Grant Street, is an old graveyard which would have fallen within the boundaries of the fort ramparts. Records from 1840 state that the foundations of an old chapel were found whilst digging graves. Little is known about the chapel, but it has been suggested that it was dedicated to St Aethan. Nothing remains of the chapel, but two fragments of stone slabs were recovered and are now on display in the Visitor Centre: the first piece shows a section of Celtic knotwork, and the second shows a hunting scene, featuring a deer.

In the old graveyard, headstones protrude from the ground at jaunty angles, some bearing fascinating memento mori carvings. The oldest legible grave is that of Robert Shaw, dated 1689. Set into the north wall is a curious stone slab onto which a pillar has been carved, and a circular depression created. This is a knocking stone. Traditionally, a knocking stone was a bowl for the purpose of milling grain in the cavity, grinding it with another stone. There are examples of more traditional, bowl-shaped knocking stones, engraved with a cross at other Scottish chapel sites but this one is set into the wall, and seems to be unique. Locals tell that it served the purpose of being rhythmically knocked as the deceased were lowered to rest. They also say, that if you knock it today you can hear the sound of a baby crying.

Being located on a peninsula, Burghead has a varied coastline. The more exposed north coast is a must for keen rock-poolers. Known locally as the backshore, at low tide rocky sandstone formations are exposed and the remaining seawater pools are full of life. Get on your wellies and see what you can find: small creatures such as sticklebacks, anemones, crabs, and starfish all make their homes in these temporary habitats.

The rocky outcrops also make handy resting places and feeding grounds for many seabirds. Orange-legged oyster-catchers scuttle among the rocks feeding on mussels which are in plentiful supply, whilst cormorants and shags perch with their wings out-spread in the sunshine, drying off their plumage.

Situated on the backshore, away from the headland is the Burghead Maltings. Established in 1966, the Diageo-owned facility doubled in size in 1971 and is at the very start of the whisky making process as within the walls of the building are 48 enormous drums used to malt the barley to specific degrees of peatiness required by individual distilleries.

Three miles away at Roseisle, a sister malting plant was opened in 1982. A huge distillery with the capacity to produce 10 million litres of whisky annually was added to the operation in 2009, and with a biomass plant which means that it generates much of its own energy, Roseisle is Scotland's most environmentally advanced malt distillery. A network of underground pipes connects the Burghead maltings with the Roseisle maltings and distillery, and waste heat from the distilling processed is used in the running of both of the maltings.

The Burghead maltings was initially served by the railway. An old branch which ran between Burghead and Alves (where it connected to the main Inverness-Aberdeen line), was extended to the maltings enabling the delivery of grain by rail. The freight service to the Burghead maltings continued until 1992 when it was replaced – initially by sea freight, and ultimately by road transport. The line was lifted, and the railway bridge leading into the village was demolished. The area of land which was occupied by the freight railway buildings has now become the **Old Railway Yard Community Garden** – a colourful splash of life where anyone can pop by and lend a hand sowing and planting whilst the kids play in the mud kitchen. Quite often there is hot food take-away service on site so once you have worked up an appetite you can indulge in a hog roast, a decadent burger, or just have a tasty coffee to enjoy on one of the garden benches.

The sheltered south coast of Burghead is an ideal location for a safe port and although the hey-day of the fishing industry has passed, the harbour here is still active with small fishing boats landing their catch of squid and shellfish, and occasional larger ships making berth there.

A monument at the harbour is dedicated to the men who lost their lives in the World War II service known as the Shetland Bus. A clandestine operation, the main role of the Shetland Bus was to create a permanent link between Mainland Shetland and Nazi-occupied Norway. Using boats which looked like fishing vessels, the allies ferried munitions, supplies and agents into Norway whilst rescuing people on the outward journey. Two such boats operated out of Burghead, and the memorial remembers those who died performing these secret missions.

Midway between the harbour and the beach is the Slappy, a sandstone slipway which makes a great spot for heading off on your canoe or paddleboard. Set back from the Slappy is a single story cottage with a carving of a salmon above the front door – the Salmon Bothy was the headquarters for the Burghead base of the Shetland Bus.

The bay at Burghead is the village's crowning glory. Stretching all the way to Findhorn is a gently sloping beach of soft pale sand, backed by banks of dunes which are held in place by swathes of marram grass, and a pine forest that is full of broad tracks which are excellent for walkers and cyclists.

At low tide, large expanses of wet sand are exposed, and you can find many beautiful seashells including delicate pastel coloured thin tellins, cockles and razor clams. Also of interest is the wreck of a barley cargo ship from 1865, and the remains of many old stakes from the days when salmon fishing was an important industry in Burghead. At the high tide mark there is a long line of concrete tank traps and several pill boxes which are the remains of WWII defences.

The Burghead Beach Caravan Park (Station Road ☎01343 830084 𝟙 BurgheadBeachCaravanPark) offers static caravans which occupy prime positions above the sand dunes with great views of the beach and the Moray Firth. Other statics are available, setback from the beach or nestled on the edge of the pine forest, and there is plenty of space for tourers and tents.

Access to the forest can be gained via the caravan park, as well as along the old railway line and at various points along the beach. Off-road parking for forest walks cans also be found at various locations on the approach to Burghead on the B9089 – this road will also lead you to the Roseisle Country Park.

CUMMINGSTON

Cummingston is a favourite spot with rock climbers. Head down to the small, pebbly beach to explore the caves and enjoy a picnic.

Known locally as *The Collach,* Cummingston is sandwiched between the fishing villages of Burghead and Hopeman. It was established in 1808 by Sir William Gordon-Cumming to house masons working in nearby stone quarries, and originally consisted of a single long street of stone cottages. Main Street was later joined by Back Street, and more recently by Seaview Road. Significantly, almost all the houses have names instead of numbers. Positioned about 131 ft (40m) above sea level, many of the homes enjoy views across the Moray Firth.

Red sandstone cliffs and stacks offer great opportunities for rock climbing and bouldering.

Where Back Street, and Seaview Road join, there is a lane leading towards the sea, where you will find parking, toilet facilities, and a popular children's play area. There is a long slide here which is possibly the best way to get down to the sea, but there are also steps if you are not feeling so adventurous.

The former railway line from Burghead to Hopeman ran just above the shoreline at Cummingston, which had its own station until 1904. The line continued to provide services to passengers until 1931, and freight including sand from local Greenbrae Quarry, eventually closing in 1957. The line has since been tarmacked and makes up part of The Moray Coast Trail, but the bridge over the line, which was to the west of the station, still stands. The trail is popular with cyclists and walkers, and the banks are lined with yellow blooming gorse, and pink fireweed. A servicing stand is provided for cyclists:

78

it is outfitted with an air pump and tools to aid changing tubes and tightening fixings.

The Collach Bay is a pebble beach, on the west side of which there are rockpools and sandstone caves to be explored at low tide.

Just to the west of the beach is an area of craggy cliffs and stacks which are favourites with climbers and boulderers. There are climbs for all abilities, and the more popular climbs have stakes at the top for abseiling. It should be noted the sandstone is soft: climbers should be aware of this and protect the cliffs from further erosion. Furthermore, extra care should be taken when using existing stakes as exposure to the elements can lead to failure of metal anchors. Do not attempt to climb the stacks without specialist equipment or supervision.

Experienced climbers can find ascent and bouldering information at UK Climbing (ukclimbing.com) where a search for 'MorayCoastGuide.pdf' links to an excellent illustrated guidebook for Cummingston and Primrose Bay.

Spectators may wish to make their way to the cliffs on a Wednesday evening when local climbing clubs are often out tackling the stacks.

For a great introduction to coastal adventures, join Outfit Moray (01343 549571 outfitmoray.com) on one of their events. They offer a huge range of organised group activities including climbing, abseiling, and coasteering.

UK Climbing lists one ascent which nearly everyone should be able to attempt without the need for specialist equipment – climbing back up the slide at the park.

HOPEMAN

The pretty little seaside village of Hopeman is easily identifiable by a row of traditional colourful beach huts on the east beach. A popular holiday destination for over a century, visitors will find lots of interest in the historic caves, two lovely beaches, and a harbour busy with pleasure boats and lobster creelers.

In June 1805, Sir Archibald Dunbar sold off some of his estate and one of those plots was bought by William Young (at the same time, Young & some partners also bought the village of Burghead). 'Lot IV: Inverugie' was little more than sand dunes, but Young had a vision, and the following year he advertised the new village of Hopeman as a desirable situation for fishermen, tradesmen, and labourers in the county of Moray. It was an immediate success – almost 70 plots were taken up, and the streets Dunbar, Farquhar, Thom, and Forsyth were named after some of these earliest inhabitants.

Enjoy designer ice-cream and search for fossilised footprints.

Young constructed a small harbour, whilst additional landing for shallow draught fishing boats was available on the west beach. The Greenbank and

Clashach quarries on either side of Hopeman provided employment and building materials for the expanding village. Young also had a lime quarry and kiln on the Inverugie Estate to the south of Hopeman from which he operated a gravity fed railway line all the way to the harbour so that the lime could be exported.

In 1819, Young sold Hopeman in order to raise the finances required to buy out the partners with whom he co-owned Burghead. Hopeman was bought by William Stuart who also owned plantations in the West Indies. Stuart improved the harbour which continued to export fish and lime, whilst the same boats delivered coal to the village. Financial difficulties forced Stuart to sell to Admiral Duff (later Vice-Admiral) of Drummuir in 1837. Duff extended the village, investing heavily in the harbour, and as a result Hopeman became one of the best fishing stations in the area. An icehouse was built circa 1854 on an area which is now the playing fields. The domed chamber was renovated as part of the village's bicentennial celebrations – new doors were fitted, and the access hatch was capped with an armillary sphere.

After the Admiral's death, Hopeman was left to his son Gordon Thomas Duff who saw yet more expansions to the harbour which were completed in 1892. At about the same time, the railway line was extended from Burghead to the Hopeman, creating an important connection between the two villages.

A mobile, hand-cranked crane was purchased for the harbour in the early 1920s. The crane was originally constructed in 1859, and it remained in use at Hopeman until 1979 where operators were able to wheel it around the harbour, lifting engines and equipment off and on fishing boats and other vessels. The crane was decommissioned and moved to its current location overlooking the harbour. In 2012 it was lovingly restored and given a coat of smart red paint.

By the 1950s the fishing industry was in decline and the railway line was closed in 1957. As with many fishing villages along the Moray coast, the decline continued and in 2008 it was decided to install pontoons at the harbour for small pleasure craft. Today, you can enjoy a walk around the harbour and see lobster creels stacked on the quayside and paddleboarders take to the water. The railway line now forms part of the Moray Coast Trail, and the tarmacked path leads all the way to Burghead.

Hopeman's harbour and beaches are at the north end of Harbour Street, along which you will find cafés and shops catering to all aspects of village life. Stew 'n' Drew serve up luxury ice cream (dairy-free and vegan options are also available), in exciting superhero combinations, and traditional flavours. Pop into Hopeman Post Office Stores to pick up seaside essentials such as a bucket and spade, or bodyboards for the more adventurous. Down by the harbour, Footprints Gallery is located on the upper level of the Harbourside Gift Shop.

The gallery hosts changing exhibitions and the gift shop is full of carefully selected crafts and gifts, many inspired by the beautiful Moray Coast.

Hopeman's smaller west beach is situated just in front of the West Beach Caravan Park (☎01343 830880 ⬛westbeachcaravanpark.co.uk). The year-round site offers quirky accommodation in cute wooden wagons and traditional static caravans, as well as pitches for tents, tourers and motorhomes. The Bootleggers Bothy (seasonal opening) is part of the park and specialises in quality take-away meals – it's hard to beat lobster fresh off the boat at Hopeman harbour.

Car parking is available behind the east beach and nearby a handy information board shows a simple map of the waterfront and what you can see there. The shoreline is populated by a row of colourful beach huts – quite an unusual feature in this part of the world – but stranger still are the fossilised prints of reptiles which pre-date the dinosaurs.

Signage indicates that between the pavilion and the first few beach huts you can find reptile prints, but the best fossils are to be found further along the coast trail at the **Clashach Quarry**.

In front of the beach huts, a natural lagoon referred to as Sheepie's Loch, provides a safe play pool for children of all ages. The changing tides ensure the water is clean: at low tide, rock pools are exposed for exploration, and when the tide is in, the pool makes for a safe swimming area.

A short walk along the coast will take you past the **Braemou Well** and up to the Clashach Quarry where you can find more fossilised evidence of creatures that once roamed this part of Moray. The narrow trail, suitable only for walkers, skirts behind the beach huts along the coast and a series of wooden signposts will keep you headed in the right direction towards Daisy Rock. A short diversion from the main trail is a path leading to the Braemou Well. Considered to have magical properties in the 1600s, the well would also have been used by early residents for their fresh water supply.

Back on the main path, you soon reach **Daisy Rock** which marks the end of Hopeman's sandy cove. Scramble up the rocky outcrop to enjoy lovely views back towards Hopeman and Burghead. At midsummer the sun sinks between Daisy Rock and its sister, Hive Rock, providing magical sunsets.

The Moray Coast Trail continues between the sea and the golf course, offering a view of the renowned Prieshach hole which overlooks a cove of the same name – the signature hole features a 100ft drop from the tee to the green. The links course was established in 1909 and the Prieshach has been rated one of the best Par 3s in Scotland by Sky Golf, and the best Par 3 ever played by Scottish golf professional Paul Lawrie OBE, winner of the Open Championship 1999, whose driver is on display in the clubhouse.

Sculptor's Cave low tide walk 8 ¼ miles max

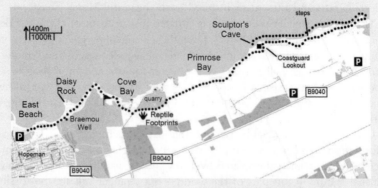

With its dark history and fascinating carvings, the Sculptor's Cave is well worth a visit. The cave is cut off at high tide so you should set off about 2½ hours before low tide to minimise the very real risk of being stranded when the tide turns. Finding the cave is an adventure in itself as you explore the coast from the top of the cliffs to the shore below.

The entrance to the cave is decorated with Pictish carvings. Excavations in 1929 uncovered evidence that the cave has been used by people from the late Bronze Age, right through to the medieval period. A significant amount of human remains was found, predominantly of children. Further excavations in the late 1970s discovered yet more human bones, and analysis in 2011 lead to the suggestion that some of the decapitated skulls were used for ritualistic purposes between the 1st and 4th century AD.

From Hopeman, follow the Moray Coast Trail past the Clashach Quarry to

Wild marsh orchids grow along this part of the coastline and are easily identified by their bright spike of purple flowers on a short stem. The path can be quite tricky to navigate with slippery boulders and prickly gorse and the trail to the quarry will start to ascend the cliffs unless you choose to take the left fork and detour down to enjoy the sheltered bay and caves at Clashach Cove.

Continue on the top path: bear left onto a track and then turn off to the right just before the entrance to the Clashach Quarry. Stone has been quarried here since the 1800s, and the sandstone at Clashach is unusually hard. The prized building material comes in different grades. The dark grade has been used in Edinburgh to give the Museum of Scotland a rich texture, whilst the modern Weston Link which joins the Scottish National Gallery with the Scottish Academy has been clad in the lightest grade of stone.

Some 250 million years ago this area was a hot dry desert, home to reptiles who left their marks in the red sandstone. Footprint and tail-drags of creatures making their way towards a fresh-water lake were preserved in the rock, and later discovered during quarrying. Many of these fossils have been removed to

Covesea Village. Half a mile from the quarry you will pass pretty Primrose Bay but as the Sculptor's Cave is only accessible at low tide it is best to press on – you can come back to Primrose Bay on your return journey. Another half mile again and you are on the headland above the Sculptor's cave: at the T-junction take the left trail towards the Covesea Coastguard Lookout Station.

Continue along the trail until you are above a small cove: looking back you may spot the access to a route down the cliffs. A series of steps have been hewn from the cliff-face and the lowest steps have been subject to erosion so you may wish to carry on to the main route and climb the steps on your return. The easy option at this stage is to follow the trail east past Covesea Village and then slightly right until you can find the intermittent paths leading down to the shore.

Head west, passing three or four headlands and navigating rocks slippery with seaweed, interspersed with sandy bays. Enjoy the spectacular scenery on the way including impressive caves, stacks, and arches carved out by the waves. Before the last headland look out for the Victorian steps cut into the rock which you may wish to use for your return. The lower steps suffer from serious erosion, but a thick rope has been installed to help tackle this section.

The Sculptor's Cave is unmissable. Set above the high tide mark, the cave has two entrances. The right entrance is partially boarded up whilst at the left entrance, Historic Scotland have added an information board to help identify the Pictish carvings. Within the cave there is a good amount of natural daylight, but a torch will help you to see the carvings which are located deeper in this historic and atmospheric cave.

Return via the cliff steps or by the original route.

If you want a shorter walk, drive towards Lossiemouth on the B9040. There is a limited amount of parking on a gated dirt track which leads to the Coastguard Lookout; and again, about ½ a mile further east of this in a small layby at an unmarked junction.

museums in Elgin, Glasgow, and Edinburgh but some of the finds are also displayed near the quarry to be enjoyed by locals.

DUFFUS

Set among rolling fields of gently swaying barley, the small, planned village of Duffus is about two miles inland from the Moray Coast Trail and can be accessed via a detour through a few trees and across some fields. The first section of this trail is less well trodden than others and you might find your legs swatted by stinging nettles. A more pleasant choice is to follow the dirt track from the Clashach Quarry to the main road then join a well-surfaced cycle path which runs parallel to the B9102 road to the village.

At the heart of the village is a small shop, catering to the needs of the community. Next door is the popular Duffus Inn where diners can enjoy fabulous views from an elevated patio, across the gently curving countryside to the dark hills of Quarry Wood. An impressive Gothic church built in 1868 dominates the western boundary of the village, whilst the east is flanked by a community park and the village hall.

A quarter of a mile to the east, along a narrow single-lane road is the charming medieval ruin of **St Peter's Kirk**. It is recommended that you walk from the village, but if you choose to drive, you can leave your car tucked into a layby just before you reach the Kirk. From here, you can access the ancient churchyard on foot, down an old, walled drive. The door of the kirk is unlocked each day so there is no need to collect the key from The Old Manse. Enter the kirk through the iron gate and old studded wooden doors of the south porch to explore inside the ruin. Steps on the outside of the kirk provide the opportunity to enjoy the church from an unusual vantage point. The steps would have been added in the 18th century to provide worshippers with access to the upper galleries when the church was remodelled in a Presbyterian style.

Explore the enchanting ruins of a medieval kirk and a hill-top castle.

The original medieval village was little more than a handful of houses. St Peter's Kirk and the moss-covered market cross within its grounds are all that remain. It was quite common to hold markets in the churchyard if that happened to be the largest available space in a village or town. The Duffus cross dates from the 1300s and situated in the sheltered grounds of the church. Wearing a mantle of green moss, it stands at its full height of over 13ft (4m).

Mature trees surround the atmospheric graveyard which is heavily populated with grave markers. Many of the moss-covered stones carry traditional symbols associated with mortality, including skulls, crossbones, and hour-glasses. It is also possible to find markers with carvings which represent the trades of those buried below.

A watchhouse in one corner was established in 1830 from which a watchman would guard fresh burials against grave robbers – a practice which ceased in 1832 when the Anatomy Act created a legitimate supply of fresh corpses for medical purposes.

A wooden church would have existed on the site post 1130, having been built to accompany Duffus Castle some two miles away. It was replaced later by a stone structure in about 1190. The roofless ruin of St Peter's was built on the foundations of the stone church. The first stone church was burned during the Scottish uprising of 1297. A new stone church was built on the original foundations and added to in subsequent years. On the south-side, a porch was added in 1524 and the carved rosettes, ribbed arch supports and pointed doorway are beautiful examples of early medieval architecture. Extensive remodelling was carried out from 1782-89 when the church was converted for Protestant worship and St Peter's Kirk continued to serve the local community until the new parish church was built to the west of the village in 1869. Abandoned for over 150 years, St Peter's Kirk still draws visitors, some of whom come to find their ancestors whilst others come out of curiosity to explore the pretty ruin of the church and unusual features of the graveyard.

Duffus Castle is the interesting ruin of a medieval stronghold which stands atop a man-made earthwork, with commanding views over the Laich. At a time when Moray was a separate kingdom to the rest of Scotland, Flemish nobleman Hugh de Freskyn was awarded the lands of Duffus and Roseisle for lending his support to the Scottish king, David I, against an uprising in 1130 which was led by the Earl of Moray. The uprising failed and Freskyn was rewarded with the earl's lands.

Freskyn built a large defensive wooden castle on top of the motte, and on a lower bailey he established a small community of supporting buildings which would have included bakehouses, a brewhouse, lodges, and stables. King David I would have stayed at Duffus castle in 1151 when he came to inspect the construction of his abbey at Kinloss. Freskyn also built the original wooden St Peter's Kirk near the medieval village of Duffus.

After Freskyn's death in 1270, ownership of Duffus Castle transferred to Sir Reginald Cheyne. In the summer of 1296, Scotland had fallen to the rule of occupation by the English king, Edward I. A key supporter of King Edward, Cheyne had accommodated a garrison of English troops at the castle, and in the summer of 1297 Duffus was destroyed by fire on the order of Andrew Murray who led the Scottish rebellion in the north of Scotland.

Gordonstoun School

Gordonstoun was founded in 1934 by the educationalist Dr Kurt Hahn. The Schule Schloss Salem – considered to be one of the most elite schools in Europe – was established by Hahn in southern Germany in 1919. A German Jew, Hahn spoke out against the Nazis and was arrested in 1933.

Lossiemouth-born Prime Minister Ramsay MacDonald exerted his influence, ensuring that Hahn was released and exiled to Britain where he set up a new school one mile east of Duffus.

As a result of Hahn's vision and reputation, the school had 135 boys in attendance by the start of WWII. Some of the students, including Prince Philip, the late Duke of Edinburgh, had transferred from Salem.

During the war years, the school was taken over by the army and used as barracks. In the years which followed, the school grew in strength and size. Outward bound activities such as seamanship and mountaineering have always been an important part of the curriculum.

Uniquely in Britain, the school has operated a part-time fire service since 1940. The campus station has two emergency fire engines, and the teams must be medically and physically fit as they attend roughly 50 call-outs a year.

Alumni include Prince Charles, the Prince of Wales, as well as several other members of the British royal family, director Duncan Jones (formerly Zowie Bowie), and the fictitious Lady Lara Croft from the Tomb Raider franchise.

Records from 1305 show that Edward granted Cheyne 200 oaks to rebuild his estate and some of these were gifted to the rector at St Peter's Kirk which had also been attacked in the uprising.

There may well have been early signs of subsidence on the motte at this stage, but nonetheless a new, more secure, three-storey castle with a grand hall was built of stone. In the broken lintels of a window on the main section you can see the huge shift in the fabric of the building, as well as evidence of repairs to the north wall of the castle tower before it dramatically slid down the motte.

Finally abandoned in the 17th century, Duffus Castle is now in the care of Historic Scotland (☐historicenvironment.scot) as is St Peter's Kirk. Both sites are free to visit and make for an interesting detour from the Moray Coast Trail.

Relax and enjoy beautiful views of Duffus Castle and the surrounding countryside with some refreshments from the cute little Kula Coffee Hut (☐KulaAtTheCastle) which serves perfect barista coffees, refreshing cold drinks, and fresh home-bakes.

As an additional unexpected treat, you may also experience the sight and sound of Typhoon fighter jets being scrambled at nearby RAF Lossiemouth. The Royal Air Force practice incredible manoeuvres as their modern jets take to the skies and whizz past the 14th century castle.

LOSSIEMOUTH

Lossiemouth (often shortened to 'Lossie') has been a popular resort for holiday makers since Victorian times. From the west beach and the iconic Covesea Lighthouse, around the busy marina with its old harbour buildings, to the quaint fishermen's cottages at Seatown and the east beach backed by pine forest, there is over three miles of stunning coastline with much to offer in terms of sports, wildlife, local history, and the popular Lossiemouth

Lossiemouth, 'the jewel of Moray' was home to the first Labour Prime Minister, Ramsay MacDonald.

Raft Race – a fun charity event held in August each year.

As with many larger towns, Lossiemouth is an amalgamation of smaller villages, namely Stotfield, Branderburgh, and Seatown, which have slowly fused together over the years. On the west side of town, Stotfield was just a farming-and-fishing hamlet in the Middle Ages, with the fishing boats landing on the sandy hythe.

The headland is occupied by Branderburgh with its striking Georgian villas, broad streets, and the double-basin harbour to which Lossiemouth owes much of its success.

In the east is **Seatown**, a charming area established at the end of the 17th century, populated by traditional fishermen's cottages. Separated from the sandy dunes of the east beach by the River Lossie, a wooden footbridge was constructed in 1850 from Seatown to the beach to encourage day-trippers. The bridge was a successful initiative with holidaymakers enjoying access to the beach and remained in use until July 2019 when it was closed due to safety concerns. Plans are underway to replace the iconic footbridge, but until such time as it is complete, access to the east beach is limited to those who can make it under their own paddle-power, or on foot for a mile and a half through the pine forest from Arthur's Bridge at Inchbroom.

Several harbours were built over the years. In 1765, the first 'harbour' made use of the mouth of the River Lossie: a jetty was constructed on the west bank of the inlet, whilst a wooden pier was built on the east of the river mouth. Today the west bank forms part of a delightful seaside promenade with generous banks of colourful flowerbeds on one side, and views across to the silvery sands of the beach, and the skeletal remains of the old wooden pier on the other.

The river harbour was busy, and so it followed that the Branderburgh harbours were established with work starting in 1837 to construct a single basin harbour. As with many coastal locations, Lossiemouth prospered with the herring boom and in 1852 the railway was extended from Elgin to cater for the demand, and over the next eight years a new large basin was added to the harbour. During this period of economic boom, the village of Branderburgh established itself with a large central square and substantial houses belonged to the successful fishermen, whilst larger villas in the south of the area belonged to businessmen.

On the edge of Seatown, at 1 Gregory Place, is the small and unassuming cottage which was the birthplace of **Ramsay MacDonald**, the UK's first Labour prime minister. Born in 1866, MacDonald's parents worked on a farm in Alves, but they weren't married and separated shortly after his birth.

A talented scholar, MacDonald left Lossiemouth for Bristol at the age of 19 where he joined a radical socialist party. A year later he moved to London where he spent some time studying at Birbeck before ill health forced him to quit his studies.

Finding employment as private secretary to the radical Liberal politician Thomas Lough was a key moment in his career, opening many doors, but it was whilst working as a freelance journalist that he really started to get involved in politics. In 1894 MacDonald stood in his first election for the Independent Labour Party, and by 1906 he was elected as MP for Leicester. During this time he met and married Margaret Gladstone, with whom he had six children.

In 1909, MacDonald had a house built for his mother. 'The Hillocks' at 17 Moray Street is less than six blocks from where he was born, and is quite unusual in that it has been built with the rear of the house facing the street. Sadly, MacDonald lost his mother in 1910 and his wife in 1911, but The Hillocks remained the family home.

MacDonald first became prime minister in 1924, and again in 1929. His governments improved housing for low-paid workers, appointed the first female cabinet minister Margaret Bondfield, raised unemployment income, and improved the conditions and wages for miners. In 1935 poor health forced MacDonald's resignation as prime minister although he remained an active member of the Labour Party until he passed away in November 1937.

The house is still lived in by MacDonald's granddaughter. Much of it still looks as it did in 1924, and it contains delightful mementos including MacDonald's school books and a pencil-written note from Mahatma Gandhi. The Hillock was a retreat from political life, but also where MacDonald worked late into the night, putting together his first cabinet.

At **Lossiemouth Fisheries and Community Museum** (Pitgaveny Street ☎01343 813772 ⊘lossiemuseum.co.uk ⊙seasonal) you can see Ramsay MacDonald's study, which has been reconstructed at the museum due to the kind donation of his family. Located by the marina and occupying two floors in an old fishing storage warehouse, this community museum was opened in 1984 after much hard work by its dedicated volunteers. Another of the fascinating exhibits are the housing gears and perfectly polished Parisian crystal lenses of the Covesea Lighthouse, and of course Lossiemouth's connection to its fishing heritage is woven through the narrative of the displays, including model fishing boats and a replica wheelhouse. The friendly volunteers help bring the exhibits to life with their stories of life in Lossie and on the sea.

Just along from the museum, is the popular Harbour Lights Café (5 Pitgaveny Quay ☎01343 814622 ⊘theharbour-lights.co.uk). Open daily until 4pm, the café also offers a bistro service on Saturday evenings. Expect fresh seafood and enjoy a mouth-watering crayfish & mango salad with a Scottish raspberry dressing, or a tasty jambalaya featuring plump prawns and chorizo. From a smoked salmon breakfast, to light lunches, delicious cakes, and an evening meal, this popular café has it covered.

From Lossiemouth Marina, you can head off out to sea on a wildlife watching trip with North 58° (page 32) with experts who can share their knowledge about the Moray Firth wildlife including dolphins, seals, and ospreys.

The beaches of Lossiemouth are without a doubt two of its best features, and each is served by a different caravan park depending on your preference.

The main access to the west beach is by a road which runs down behind the grand club house of Moray Golf Club to a public parking area where there is a café and public toilet. Founded in 1889 the club offers two courses, the old course being one of the finest links courses in Scotland. Famous alumni include Meg Farquhar (1910-1988) Britain's first professional female golfer, and Ramsay MacDonald who had his membership revoked in 1915 due to his anti-war stance.

The beach is separated from the links course by a bank of sand dunes held in place by marram grass and yellow-blooming gorse. The start of the bay sweeps around in a broad curve and is best accessed at low tide when acres of golden sand are revealed. At the start of the beach, a row of anti-tank defences follows the natural line of low sandstone formations, providing rockpools for shellfish and other small sea creatures.

Halfway along the bay is the rocky headland Craighead. Here, **Covesea Lighthouse** stands majestically above a series of caves which tunnel back into the rock, and a WWII pillbox still stands guard over the Moray Firth.

Completed in 1846, the lighthouse was manned until 1984 when automation meant that lighthouse keepers were no longer required. In 2012, a North Cardinal Buoy was positioned next to the Halliman Skerries, and the lighthouse lamp was switched off. Now publicly owned, the lighthouse is open to visitors, and the keepers' cottages are available as unique holiday accommodation. The cottages are tastefully decorated, and new bathroom suites have recently been installed. From your accommodation you can enjoy fabulous views across the bay which is just a short walk down a rough track.

Tours of the lighthouse operate at 11am and noon, every Saturday from Easter/the first weekend in April (whichever is earlier), to the end of October (☎01343 810664 info@covesealighthouse.co.uk). Bookings take priority so ensure that you confirm your place and discover the history of the iconic tower. Tours start with a casual introduction presented in the quarterdeck prior to climbing the 144 steps and two ladders to the top of the tower and taking a walk outside. The lighthouse architect Alexander Stephenson was responsible for most of the lighthouses in Scotland. Attention to detail in design elements include ornate handles in the form of serpents which surround the platform the crew would have stood on to clean the exterior of the glass housing.

Situated near Covesea Lighthouse is the **RAF & Fleet Air Arm Heritage Centre** (☎01343 835537 ⊙Easter/April-October Sat & Sun 11am-4pm). Staffed by volunteers who are all former armed-forces personnel, the centre is full of history and artefacts associated with Lossiemouth's military connection. A wall-mounted timeline depicts the aircraft and services which have operated from the base since 1939. Old technology is on display next to modern equipment including a submarine-detecting sonobuoy which is suspended from the ceiling.

Enthusiasts can rifle through shelves of technical books and folders containing information about squadrons which have served from the base. Various uniforms are displayed on mannequins whilst others are available for dressing-up fun. Detailed model aircraft are exhibited in glass cases and there is an impressive large-scale model of an aircraft carrier. The fact that the staff served locally means that you get first-hand knowledge of the roles played by the local service bases in protecting the UK from threats including Russian submarines.

Typhoons and Poseidon aircraft fly on exercises from RAF Lossiemouth on a daily basis. Exercises are not announced but if you drive around the perimeter of the airbase you may well see several vehicles parked up as people take time to catch the spectacle of the agile Typhoons perform impressive take-offs and scream through the skies.

The miles of soft sands and dunes of the east beach has limited public access until the new bridge is open but if you are feeling adventurous you can hire a paddleboard from New Wave Surf (page 29) located in The Old School House – a reclaimed out-building with an aged, corrugated roof, located on the East Beach Car Park, close to the footbridge. Paddle the estuary to the dunes and enjoy sharing this beautiful beach with the other lucky few who have been willing to make the effort. The east beach stretches for ten miles to Kingston on Spey where the golden sands are replaced by stones and shingle which have been brought down to the coast by the powerful waters of the River Spey. Depending on the conditions, and your skills, you may want to tackle some of the surf breaks – or just enjoy a relaxing paddle whilst keeping an eye out for the local dolphins.

It is generally agreed that a beer tastes best when you have earned it, so after a hard day on the beach you could treat yourself to a locally made craft beer at the Windswept Brewing Company (Unit B, 13 Coulardbank Industrial Estate ☎01343 814310 🌐windsweptbrewing.com). The Windswept Brewery was started by two former RAF pilots who decided they wanted to make Lossiemouth their home. The brewery has an onsite bar called the Tap Room and they produce a range of traditional and modern beers, some – *Hurricane, Typhoon, Poseidon* – are named to reflect aviation history, whilst there are interesting collaborations with Glen Moray Distillery to produce dark ales that are aged in whisky casks. Sign up for a fun tour and tasting session (two flights of dark, light, and amber ales) with the friendly Tap Room manger Andrew, or just relax at the bar and enjoy a wood-fired pizza with your pint.

SPEYSIDE

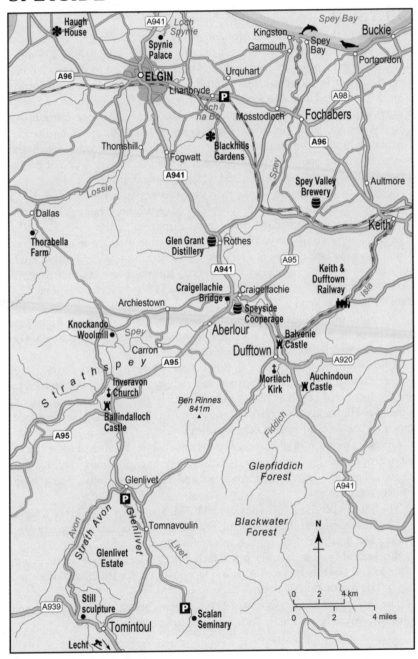

Haugh House

Loch Spynie

A941

Spey Bay

Kingston
Garmouth
Spey Bay

Buckie

Portgordon

Spynie Palace

ELGIN

Urquhart

A96

Lhanbryde

P

A98

Mosstodloch

Fochabers

Thomshill

Fogwatt

Blackhills Gardens

Loch na Bo

A96

A941

Lossie

Spey

Spey Valley Brewery

Aultmore

Dallas

Thorabella Farm

Glen Grant Distillery

Rothes

Keith

A941

A95

Keith & Dufftown Railway

Isla

Craigellachie Bridge

Craigellachie

Archiestown

Speyside Cooperage

Knockando Woolmill

Spey

Aberlour

Balvenie Castle

Carron

Strathspey

A95

Dufftown

A920

Inveravon Church

Mortlach Kirk

Auchindoun Castle

Ben Rinnes 841m

Ballindalloch Castle

A95

Fiddich

Glenfiddich Forest

Glenlivet

A941

Avon

P

Strath Avon

Glenlivet

Tomnavoulin

Blackwater Forest

N

Livet

Glenlivet Estate

Still sculpture

A939

P

Scalan Seminary

0   2   4 km

0   2   4 miles

Tomintoul

Lecht

SPEYSIDE

High in the Monadhliath Mountains, the River Spey begins at the outlet of Loch Spey. It is the third-longest river in Scotland, channelling 107 miles through rugged whisky country to the coast, five miles west of Buckie. Rainfall and snow-melt in the mountains contribute to making it the fastest-flowing river in Scotland. The entire length of the River Spey is designated as a Site of Special Scientific Interest owing to the populations of Atlantic salmon, sea lamprey, otters, and rare freshwater pearl mussels to be found there. Historically, trees from forests at Aviemore and Aberlour were felled, and floated down the Spey for ship-building at Kingston on Spey – and of course it is important for salmon fishing and whisky production.

Speyside produces more whisky than any other region in the world, and over half of Scotland's distilleries are here. The Malt Whisky Trail celebrates this heritage with a recommended list of eight distilleries, and a cooperage. The cooperage and five of the distilleries are in Speyside, two are in the Laich of Moray, and the Dallas Dhu is a historic distillery museum near Forres. There are over 50 working distilleries in Speyside, and these are celebrated in the week-long Spirit of Speyside Whisky Festival which is held over the May Day Bank Holiday weekend.

The Spirit of Speyside also celebrates 'Distilled: Food and Drink' in the first weekend of September and has plans to continue the success of the new Gin Experience which was held at Castle Gordon.

Along with fresh salmon and single malt whisky, Speyside is home to Walker's Shortbread. Scottish heritage and industry are further exemplified by the production of tweed at Knockando Woolmill, and traditional pageantry at numerous Highland games festivals every summer. In winter, exhilarating snow sports can be enjoyed at the Lecht ski resort.

Getting around by public transport is tricky, but the main bus is the 36 service operated by Stagecoach (stagecoachbus.com) from Dufftown to Elgin, calling at Craigellachie, Aberlour and Rothes en route. There is no Sunday service.

The Moray Bluebird (moray.gov.uk) 365 bus leaves Tomintoul daily at 7.55am for Keith via Aberlour and Dufftown on Tuesday, Thursday, and Friday. The return service leaves Keith at 4.30pm.

Bluebird also runs the 366 bus which operates one return service on a Monday and Wednesday from Aberlour at 9.05am via Knockando, Rothes and Elgin. The return journey departs Elgin at 1.20pm.

The Dial M for Moray (0300 1234565) is available Monday to Friday and must be booked by phone by 3pm the day before travel.

SPEY BAY WILDLIFE RESERVE

Several small communities occupy the banks on either side of the mouth of the River Spey as it flows into the Moray Firth. On the east side where the Spey meets the sea is Tugnet, and just next to this is Spey Bay which stretches east to the Spey Bay Golf Club and upriver to the big old iron railway bridge (now a footbridge), which crosses the Spey.

Learn about our marine mammals at the Scottish Dolphin Centre.

West of the bridge is Garmouth, and less than mile downstream is Kingston on Spey, with the Garmouth & Kingston Golf Course in between them. These villages surround an incredible nature reserve and Site of Special Scientific Interest, covering 1,100 acres.

As the fast-flowing waters of the Spey come tumbling down from the Monadhliath mountain range, they bring with them vast quantities of stones. Working with the waves and the wind, nature has transformed these stones into Scotland's largest shingle beach – an ideal breeding ground for common and arctic terns.

Away from the shore, the broad estuary of the Spey forms salt-marshes which provide important habitats for many species of butterfly including the small blue, grayling, and dingy skipper. Wading birds such as the common redshank and bar-tailed godwits are frequent visitors, feeding on small invertebrates in the mudflats.

The Spey is a popular hunting ground for ospreys from April through to September. Nearly driven to extinction due to the fanaticism of Victorian egg collectors, this iconic bird of prey has made a significant recovery. A large raptor with brown wings spanning 71-inches (180cm) and a white body, look out for these spectacular birds diving towards the Spey, and stretching out their talons to scoop the fish out of the water.

Keep an eye out for otters fishing and playing by the riverbanks. These shy animals are best spotted at dawn and dusk and up near the old railway bridge is a recommended location.

Common and grey seals can be seen basking on the beach at low tide as they wait for their food to go down, or bobbing about in the waters of the Firth. The common seal is smaller than the grey seal, and ironically, less common. Both species are generally grey in colour with dark spots, although the common seal can range in colour from blonde to black. The best way to distinguish one from the other is that the common seal has a shorter snout with a rounder, 'cuter' face, whilst the grey seal's head is longer, with a sloping hook nose profile.

The real star of the show here is the dolphin, and the Moray Firth is home to the world's largest bottlenose dolphins. Whales, porpoises, and dolphins are collectively known as cetaceans, and although more than 20 species of animals from this group live in Scottish waters, only seven species live close to the coast. The Moray Firth supports the only known resident population of bottlenose dolphins in the North Sea, and because of this it has been granted Special Area of Conservation status to help protect these beautiful creatures. There are several locations where dolphins are regularly spotted: these are Burghead, Hopeman, and Spey Bay – but you can spot them all along the Moray Coast. At nearly 13ft (3.9m) long, the Scottish bottlenose dolphin is 30% larger than its Caribbean counterpart, but just as graceful – and watching them jump and breach is an exciting experience.

Other aquatic visitors to the Moray Firth include, harbour porpoises, minke whales, basking sharks, and even orca, and you can learn all about these amazing animals at the **Scottish Dolphin Centre** (Spey Bay ℂ01343 820339 ⊕dolphincentre.whales.org). Run by Whale and Dolphin Conservation, the leading charity dedicated to the protection of whales and dolphins, the centre occupies part of an 18th-century salmon fishing station which has a fascinating history. Entry is free and the staff and volunteers offer land-based dolphin watching experiences and guided wildlife walks as well as bookable small group tours to their exhibition space which is packed with educational material and a fantastic collection of whale bones from the local area. The gift shop is well stocked with fair trade items and includes everything from plush toy dolphins to stylish clothing and hand-crafted gifts, whilst the café sells light lunches and tempting cakes which can be enjoyed on the nearby picnic benches. You can also book a tour of the Tugnet Icehouse.

Comprised of three long, brick-vaulted chambers, covered by curving turf roofs, **Tugnet Icehouse** is an unusual looking structure. Built in 1830 it is the largest surviving icehouse in the United Kingdom and only the upper third is visible above ground. Each winter, ice would be gathered from special ponds and tipped into the deep chambers so that fish could be stored prior to being packed in ice, and shipped south (initially by sea, and latterly by rail), to London and other markets.

Commissioned by the Duke of Gordon, the salmon fishery generated considerable income for the Gordon Castle estates, and employment for the local community. In 1792, as many as 24 ships left the fishery, London-bound, and loaded with salmon. Over 150 people were employed at the fishery, including coopers and overseers. The fishermen used stake nets and cobles – a type of open traditional fishing boat with a flat bottom which was designed for salmon fishing off beaches. The icehouse was still being used in 1968 but the hey-day of Tugnet had been and gone. In the early 1960s, the number of days the men were allowed to fish the river was gradually reduced due to an agreement between the Crown Estate and those who owned the riverbank which curtailed the net fishing of salmon, thus allowing more salmon to move up-river to the fishing beats where angling is controlled by permits.

Today, the Tugnet Icehouse can be visited on an enjoyable small group tour. Priced at just £15 for a maximum of six people, a friendly guide will escort you inside the cool chambers of the icehouse and talk about a series of displays about the salmon fishing industry and the local wildlife, including a collection of huge bones from sea mammals.

The communities on either side of the Spey are linked at Garmouth and Spey Bay by the Spey Viaduct. Formerly a railway viaduct which was used by trains operating between Aberdeen and Elgin, this huge Victorian steel bridge is now a footpath and has been incorporated into the Moray Coastal Trail. Opened in 1886 the bridge has an impressive span of 950ft (290m) to enable it to contend with changing channels of the broad mouth of the River Spey, and the graceful curve of the central bowed truss is 42ft (13m) at its highest point.

On the west bank of the Spey, the narrow rambling streets of Garmouth make a pleasant contrast to the handsome planned villages you find across Moray. Once a significant shipping port which specialised in treating and exporting timber, Garmouth has an ancient charter which entitles it to hold one of the longest surviving fairs in Scotland. Maggie Fair has been held annually on the last Saturday in June since 1587, and visitors come to enjoy an afternoon of shopping, sideshows, and entertainment.

Kingston had been a quiet village but in 1785 a shipyard opened, utilising the Spey to float an entire forest down from Aviemore. At the peak of activity between the 1850s and 1870s, there were seven shipyards located in the village, turning out everything from fishing smacks to tea clippers. In all, over 300 ships were built, and some of the last were steam drifters just before the outbreak of World War I. Ultimately the timber shipyards couldn't compete with steel, and the vibrant local industry disappeared.

The large bank of shingle to the west of the village is known as the Lein and it makes up part of the Spey Bay Wildlife Reserve. From 1935, gravel mining extracted much of the bare shingle from the Lein. There was also a stone-crushing and pre-cast concrete plant here which closed in 1960 due to severe flooding. Along the shingle bay, as well as the anti-tank concrete pillars and pillboxes which are commonplace on the Moray Coast, you will see horizontal bollards which are part of the flood defences.

Once again, Kingston is a quiet village: industry has gone; the shingle beach has returned, and with it, rare plants and animals. The yellow flowers of kidney vetch are the only source of food for caterpillars of the protected small blue butterfly, and bright patches of this important plant grow on the shingle.

There are two car parks at Kingston – east and west – the former being a favourite with birdwatchers as it provides the perfect observation point across the saltmarshes and out to sea. From May to August, when terns are nesting, you are requested not to walk on the shingle; and at all times, you should try not to park on vegetated land.

On weekdays, Garmouth and Kingston are served by the 334 bus service from Elgin and then it is just a pleasant 1½ miles on foot to the Tugnet

Baxters of Speyside

In 1868, a new grocery shop opened in Fochabers: 25-year old George Baxter had left his job as a gardener at Gordon Castle and borrowed some money from family members to set up a new business. In the back of the shop, George's wife Margaret would make delicious fruit jams – a hit with the duke and his guests, these tasty preserves became a staple at Gordon Castle.

Nearly 50 years later, the couple's son William bought some land from the duke and built a factory near the banks of the Spey. Ethel created a range of fine jams, and William travelled all over Scotland marketing them. The business also started to produce canned fruit.

Ethel first produced Baxters famous Royal Game soup in 1929, and orders came flooding in from fine food halls including Harrods and Fortnum & Mason.

The company continued to trade during the Second World War, largely by producing jam for the armed forces. After the war William and Ethel's sons, Gordon and Ian took over the family business. In 1952 Gordon's wife Ena, a talented cook and artist, turned her hand to creating a new range of Scottish soups including Cock-a-leekie and Scotch Broth, setting the foundations for the global Baxters empire.

The company went from strength to strength. In the 1950s George and Ena spent time in America building the brand's reputation. The honour of Royal Warrants was bestowed in 1955, and by the end of the decade the company had achieved global success.

Baxters became the first company in the UK to use twist-top caps when they started using them on their preserve jars in 1962.

Ena Baxter's friendly face became synonymous with the brand when she started appearing on UK TV adverts in the 1970s, lovingly tending the stockpot in the kitchen of the family home. Baxters also became the nation's largest producer of beetroot products.

Ena and Gordon continued to experiment with new flavours, ensuring the continuing success of the luxury soup brand around the world. Their daughter Audrey took over as managing director in 1992.

Audrey became the fourth generation of the family to head the firm and under her management Baxters acquired other businesses including meat pie maker Fray Bentos in 2011.

In 2018, Baxters celebrated its 150th anniversary.

The company now manufactures food in Canada, Australia, Poland, and the United States. They produce classic chutneys, designer deli-style pickles, and luxury conserves alongside modern and traditional soups in a bid to live up to the words of George Baxter: 'Be different, be better'.

Icehouse through the nature reserve and across the viaduct, making use of the Moray Coast Trail and the Speyside Way. Alternatively, use the Dial M for Moray on-demand bus service, (ensure you book before 3pm the day before you travel).

FOCHABERS

The charming village of Fochabers was originally located a bit further north, on a section of land which is now part of the Walled Garden of Gordon Castle. A new town was founded in 1776 by Alexander Gordon, the 4th Duke of Gordon, moving Fochabers a bit further away from his castle, and establishing a town, the centre of which is now a conservation area. From West Street to East Street, and South Street to Castle Street, many of the buildings on the High Street are listed as being of historical or architectural interest. The high street used to be part of the busy A96, and traffic would come thundering through - thankfully, a bypass was opened in 2012 and Fochabers can be explored in relative peace.

Fochabers has a long connection with Scottish fiddle music. William Marshall (1748-1833) was born there and is recognised as one of Scotland's greatest fiddle composers of Strathspey reels. James Alexander MBE (b. 1955) is widely acknowledged as a leading fiddle musician and teacher of traditional Scottish music. For nearly forty years, Alexander taught in schools, during which time he established the Fochabers Fiddlers, and launched Speyfest.

A friendly village museum, award-winning ice cream, and a festival of fiddle music.

The Fochabers Fiddlers was started in 1980 as an initiative to get young musicians interested in Scottish music. The group, which was made of up pupils from Milne's High School and fronted by Alexander and other experienced fiddlers, had international success.

In late July, **Speyfest** (speyfest.com) celebrates traditional and Celtic music with a mixture of concerts, ceilidhs, and workshops held over three days. The festival has been running since 1996, and attracts world-class musicians, as well as providing a platform for up-and-coming artists.

Fochabers is a stop on the long distance trail, The Speyside Way but it also features lots of well-signposted short walks by the banks of the river and through the forest. Visit forestryandland.gov.scot to download maps for the Winding Walks – a series of four forest trails running through the 19th-century gardens which belonged to the Duke and Duchess of Gordon. Shorter walks such as the Fochabers Burn, the Belt Path, and Behind the Green Door can be downloaded from morayways.org.

Gordon Castle

> Give me the stream that sweetly laves,
> The banks by Castle Gordon

Robert Burns Castle Gordon 1787

There has been a castle here since 1479. In the 16th century, the original fortress was extended to become a magnificent Renaissance mansion with majestic towers and turrets. The 4th Duke of Gordon then rebuilt the castle in 1769 on a monumental scale. One of the largest buildings in Scotland, Gordon Castle is a Scottish Versailles, with landscaped park gardens in the style of Lancelot 'Capability' Brown, and a walled garden built with stones from Burghead.

Generations of Gordons enjoyed hosting many important guests including the poet Robert Burns, and The Prince of Wales (George V). Gordon Castle Games were established by the 7th Duke in the early 20th century and crowds in excess of 20,000 would come to see world records be broken.

The games were revived in 1976 as a one-off special to celebrate Fochabers' bi-centennial, and later re-established as an annual event in 2011 when the first Gordon Castle Highland Games and County Fair took place.

During the First World War, the castle was used as a military hospital, and in the Second World War it was occupied by troops.

The tenure of the 8th Duke lasted only seven years, and in 1938, the 9th Duke was forced to sell the castle to the Crown Estate in order to settle the crippling death duties of two deceased dukes.

Years of occupation by military troops, and successive harsh winters resulted in rot, and damp taking hold of the central block of the castle. The Crown Estate

The layout for Fochabers centres on a large grass square, and Bellie Kirk (7 the Square ☎01343 820256 🖳bellieandspeymouth.org.uk) is the Alexander Gordon's centrepiece for the village. The Georgian neo-classical church has a portico supported by four pillars – the first of its kind in the Scotland. A square tower rises above the portico and features a clock face from 1798. The tower is topped by an octagonal belfry. To celebrate the church's bi-centennial, a trilogy of stained glass windows by Shona McInnes was installed. The Bellie Church is open to the public on selected Friday, Saturday, and Sunday afternoons.

The large cast-iron fountain on The Square is dedicated to the 6th Duke of Richmond and Gordon in 1878 for supplying water to the town.

Built in 1834, **Gordon Chapel** (40 Castle Street ☎01542 882782 🖳islaspeydevoran-churches.org) features the largest collection of Pre-Raphaelite stained glass windows in Scotland. Five of the windows were designed by Edward Burne-Jones, and made by Morris & Co., the firm created by the designer William Morris. They have beautiful backgrounds of intertwining branches and flora. As well as these, two windows bear the coat decided to sell Gordon Castle, and it was bought by Sir George Gordon Lennox, grandson of the 7th Duke. The decision was made to demolish the central block and convert the east wing into a comfortable family home.

Since 2008, Gordon Castle has been home to Angus Gordon Lennox, great-great-grandson of the 7th Duke, and his wife Zara. Under their management a variety of enterprises have been launched. Cottages within the estate have been converted to holiday lets; the castle is now a wedding venue; fly fishing is available on eight beats of the Spey; and although Gordon Castle is not open for visitors, it is available on an exclusive hire basis with a resident gourmet chef, from £5,500 per night (☎01343 820 244 ⌨gordoncastle.co.uk).

The eight-acre **Walled Garden** is located south of the castle. The gardens have been restored and designed to be as beautiful as they are productive. A busy team of staff tend a variety of herbs, flowers, fruit, and vegetables. Ciders are made from apples and pears; gin is infused with garden botanicals; and fresh produce is used in the award-winning café.

The beautiful and busy gardens are open all year round for visitors to enjoy. The shop sells seasonal produce and cut flowers from the gardens and luxury items which contain elements from the estate such as raspberry shortbread, and smoked rock salt which has a hint of chilli to it.

There is also a play area on site which has been designed to encourage children to explore and understand their natural environment. Entry to the gardens and play area is charged, with the entry fee going towards the ongoing restoration project (☎01343 612317 ⌨gordoncastle.co.uk).

Although Gordon Castle is not open to visitors, a variety of events are held in the picturesque grounds including the **Gordon Castle Highland Games and Country Fair** in May, live music, and outdoor cinema evenings.

of arms for two members of the Gordon family, and two modern windows were added in the following centuries.

In 1990, the Scottish artist Crear McCartney was commissioned to create a window depicting St Andrew, in memory of Sir George Gordon Lennox and he continued the organic theme which is featured in the Morris & Co. windows.

The 2003 Baxter window commemorates William and Ethel Baxter. It was created by Petri Anderson of Chapel Studio, Herefordshire, and contains design elements suggested by the Baxters' sons Gordon and Ian. The central motif of Jesus and the Fishermen is set against the backdrop of the River Spey at the Earth Pillars above the Aultdearg Burn, and local wildlife in the composition includes an osprey and salmon.

The Chapel was almost sold to house a cinema in 1948, but the congregation of less than ten people managed to raise the funds to buy the building, and Ethel Baxter was pivotal in the campaign.

Fochabers Folk Museum and Heritage Centre (22 High Street ☎01343 821204 ⨍thehistoryplace) was established by a small group of people who wanted to collect and preserve photographs and documents relating to the history and heritage of Fochabers and the surrounding area. This small ambition has resulted in a treasure trove of quirky exhibits including an old school room, a Victorian kitchen, and a shop. Housed in the former Pringle Church, there are lots of hands-on experiences and the upstairs space has a mini-transport museum with 19th-century carriages. Entry is free and donations are welcome.

Watt's Antiques (45 High Street ☎01343 820077 🖥wattsantiques.com) is a family run business dealing in everything from jewellery to furniture and Persian carpets. The building itself is of no great significance, but the windows of the shop showcase some of the fine porcelain figurines, clocks, and curiosities, and inside there are many desirable pieces of jewellery.

Milne's Primary School (59 High Street) is a very grand Neo-Tudor building with crenellations, ornate pinnacles, and detailed octagonal turrets. Its benefactor, Alexander Milne, was born in Fochabers in 1742 and held a position as footman at Gordon Castle. When the Duke asked Milne to powder his red hair, Milne quit his employment, and emigrated to America. By 1776 he was living in New Orleans, and after doing well in the hardware business, he set up a brick-making company using mainly slave labour. He had huge success: most of the brick used in New Orleans in the 18th century was made at his works, and he invested heavily in land.

When Milne died at the age of 96, his will included $100,000 for the provision of a free school in Fochabers, as well as establishing orphanages in Milneburg; bequeathing money to existing institutions in La Fayette; and freeing his two house servants, making a provision for them to have houses built. Louisiana courts twice ruled against the legacy, and the Duke of Gordon brought lengthy litigation which he finally won, and Milne's Free School was built in 1846.

Food & Drink

Fochabers Ice Cream Parlour 33-35 High Street ☎01343 829128 🖥fochabersicecream.co.uk

Winner of *Scotland's Best Ice Cream Parlour* in 2016, this sweet treat café is open daily, and offers 26 flavours of indulgent ice cream, handmade on the premises by Sheila. On a rainy day, enjoy a luxury hot chocolate and delicious home-baking inside the café, or if the sun is out, take your ice cream away and sit in The Square.

Fochabers Fish Bar 19 High Street ☎01343 820 320 🖥fochabersfishbar.co.uk

Scotland's No1 Fish and Chip Takeaway 2017 also provides seating for diners. Freshly made to order - if you want chips with your fish, ask for a 'fish supper' - or maybe you'd rather try haggis, dipped in a light batter and deep fried to crisp perfection.

A.J. Jamieson Butcher 1 Duke Street ☎01343 821

If you are self-catering, pop into this Scottish Craft Butcher and pick up something special for dinner. Indulge in melt-in-the-mouth black garlic fillet steaks, salt & pepper chicken balls, or pick up a barbecue pack to make the most of the long Scottish summer evenings.

ROTHES

Rothes Visitor Centre 86 New Street ☎01340831474
⌨rothesvisitorcentre.scot
⊙Easter-Christmas Mon-Fri 11am-3pm, Sat 10am-noon

Rothes is a small but busy town on the west bank of the Spey which is home to no less than four distilleries. On a green mound at the south end of Rothes are the remains of a castle which was one of the most powerful of medieval fortresses.

There had been a settlement here as long ago as 600AD, but modern Rothes dates from 1763 when it was announced that the Earl of Findlater intended to develop the village by selling feus (plots), and plans were established for a crofting township.

Of all the distilleries which call Rothes home – Speyburn, Glen Grant, Glen Spey, and Glenrothes – only **Glen Grant** (☎01340 832118 ⌨glengrant.com) is open to visitors and even if you aren't partial to whisky, the wonderful gardens are free to visit. Arriving in Rothes from the north, you are greeted by a large white sign pointing you in the direction of the Glen Grant Distillery and Garden.

Visit Glen Grant Distillery, and indulge in fine food at the Station Hotel.

Set midway through the Malt Whisky Trail, Glen Grant was established in the 1840s by brothers John and James Grant, who already had experience in illegal distilling and smuggling.

Water for this single malt comes from the Back Burn, and James Grant decided to celebrate the importance of this key ingredient by creating beautiful gardens in 22 acres of the glen formed by the burn. The walk through the Victorian gardens commences with a trail through sweet-smelling woodland, before opening up to spacious orchards. Once over the bridge, tall pines flank one side of the pathway whilst the other side leads to a pond bursting with lilies.

Pink primula, banked by mature rhododendron bushes skirt around the edge of a meadow. At the end of the meadow is the star attraction of the gardens: a raised, rustic wooden walkway, cross-crossing over the burn as it flows through a luscious ferny gorge. Unique features include The Dram Pavilion where Major

James Grant (the second generation owner) would entertain distillery guests, and a cave where a cask of the distillery's finest whisky is safely stored behind locked bars.

As children under eight years are not allowed on the Glen Grant distillery tour, these gardens also feature an animal trail so children can enjoy exploring them with an adult who might wish to join them. The gardens are an unexpected attraction at a distillery and an integral part of the Glen Grant story. There is no charge if you want to explore the gardens without going on a distillery tour, and the gardens are accessed through the visitor centre. Teas, coffees and cakes can be enjoyed on the sunny paved courtyard at very fair prices, and a tasting of two generous drams is only £5.

Affectionately known as 'The Cottage', **Rothes Visitor Centre**, (86 New Street &01340 831474 🔲rothesvisitorcentre.scot), with its smart, white-painted exterior, is one of the first buildings you encounter as you arrive in Rothes from the north. The staff are local volunteers and always ready to help

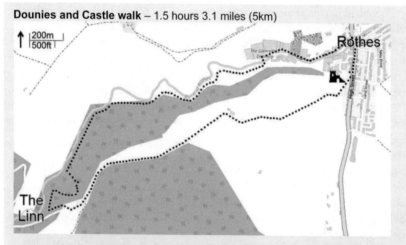

Dounies and Castle walk – 1.5 hours 3.1 miles (5km)

On the corner of Burnside Street, is Rothes Police Station. This side street will lead you to the Dounies and the Fairies Well. Although there is no fairy village on this popular walk, there is a viewing platform above the Falls of Linn of Dounie. 'Linn' is a Scottish word which means 'waterfall' and can also be used to refer to the pool of water at the foot of a waterfall. To get to the Fairies Well, turn right onto Burnside Street. Ignore the sign which directs you over a footbridge towards the castle, and continue past the graveyard, and the main entrance to the Glenrothes Distillery. You will find a signpost for Dounie and Fairies Well directing you to cross a footbridge over the Burn of Rothes. Once over the bridge, turn right and follow the burn for half a mile.

however they can. As well as a selection of cards and gifts, The Cottage also provides internet and toilet facilities.

Toots Café Bar & Bistro offers a modern Scottish dining experience for both visitors and guests at the four star **Station Hotel** (51 New Street ☎01340 832200 🖰stationhotelspeyside.com). The décor of the handsome Victorian building is reflective of the rich heritage of the local area. The light and airy Toots Bar is furnished with copper details evocative of the whisky stills; the Spirit Safe is an intimate bar well stocked with golden liquid treasure; and luxurious tartan touches are used throughout.

Pop in for an early morning coffee or come back later for a main meal. The menu features local specialities including buffalo dishes with meat sourced from the Thorabella herd at Dallas, goat from Elchies Estate, and bacon from Ballindalloch. The Station Hotel is a celebration of whisky, and each dish comes with a recommended dram, hand-picked from their collection of over 400 national and international whiskies.

The grassy path winds its way through the woods, occasionally deviating from the side of the burn. A signpost ('Dounie and Fairies Well') will let you know when to turn left, away from the burn and into dense forestry.

The fairies have very wisely covered their well with a manhole-cover as it is the source of water for Glenrothes Distillery. Continue along the path into the Little Dounie where the glen is a bit steeper and narrower. A steady climb for 10-15 minutes will take you to another signpost: turn right to get to the viewing platform for the Falls of Linn. Enjoy the views and a well-earned rest before heading back to the signpost and following the path ahead.

The track stays in the forest and takes you to two T-junctions – at each of these you should turn left. Shortly after the second left, you should emerge from the forest onto a track by Rothes Golf Course, (take care here in case a stray ball comes your way). Stay on the track until you reach the clubhouse, where the track becomes a narrow tarmac road. Follow this road as it sweeps across open countryside with a view of Ben Aigan ahead of you. Where the road enters a small area of woodland, you will find a signpost directing you to the castle.

Little more than part of the outer wall remains of the 13th century castle which once stood four storeys high. Within 400 years, the castle fell into disrepair and was abandoned. The derelict property became a refuge for thieves, and in 1662 the people of Rothes took it upon themselves to set fire to the castle and destroy it.

Leave the castle the way you arrived, following the road as it curves down, around the hill and back to the main road a few blocks south from where your walk began.

If you want to drive to the castle instead of taking the Dounie and Fairies Well Walk, you should take this road. As you ascend the narrow road which climbs around the hill on which the castle was built you can enjoy views across Rothes to Ben Aigan. At the top of the hill is parking for just one or two cars.

DUFFTOWN

Rome was built on seven hills,
Dufftown stands on seven stills.

Local rhyme

Malt whisky capital of the world, Dufftown was established in the ancient parish of Mortlach by James Duff, 4th Earl of Fife, as housing for soldiers returning home from the Napoleonic War in 1817. Situated in a scenic spot below the Conval Hills, and on the banks of the rivers Fiddich and Dullan Water, Dufftown was built on the grid pattern familiar to many of the towns in Moray. The main roads, Conval Street and Balvenie Street seem to be exceptionally broad and converge upon the fine clock tower which stands three storeys high. Originally built as the town gaol in 1839, it has subsequently been used as the Burgh Chambers, private accommodation, and the Tourist Office. Rumour has it that an illegal whisky distillery operated out of the clock tower in around 1900 when it was used by the Burgh Chambers but owing to the proliferation of the legal distilleries in the town, officials failed to notice any unusual smells coming from the tower. Now an unusual self-catering holiday rental, you can book your stay in the historic Dufftown Tower View (☏07803 428538 𝕗dufftowntowerview).

A heritage railway line, historic distilleries, and dramatic ruined castles.

Mortlach was the first legal distillery in Dufftown, founded in 1823 (the same year as the Excise Act), and preceding all other Dufftown distilleries by sixty years. Local man William Grant was employed at Mortlach for twenty years, rising to the position of manager. From here, he left to set up Dufftown's second distillery in 1886: Glenfiddich.

By the 1860s, Mortlach enjoyed international success, and it was expanded in 1897, implementing the unique 2.81 distillation process. The distillery was purchased by Johnnie Walker & Sons in 1923 and now, under the control of Diageo, Mortlach whiskies continue to be used in the Johnnie Walker brand, as well as in four single malt expressions.

Meanwhile, Grant was having great success with Glenfiddich and opened another distillery in an uninhabited mansion which had formerly been one of the residences of the Duke of Fife: Balvenie New House. Balvenie Distillery is one of only two distilleries in Scotland to grow and malt its own barley. The latter process is now mainly outsourced to large malting plants, mostly due to the high volumes of production in the modern whisky industry.

The name Mortlach comes from the old parish just to the south of Dufftown. In the year 566, St Moulag founded a religious community here which became one of the oldest Christian settlements in Scotland. The origins of **Mortlach Kirk** (church) date back to the 7th century, and whilst the earliest parts of the church may date back that far, there was major rebuilding in the 13th century, and again in the 19th century. Legend tells that King Malcolm II extended the church by the length of three spears after defeating the Danes in 1010.

The north wall of the church contains a leper's squint which allowed lepers to observe the altar during services without coming into contact with other worshippers. The kirkyard is full of interest: a 19th-century watch-house enabled watchmen to protect fresh graves from grave-robbers; and in the lower graveyard, a Pictish stone called the **Battle Stone** stands at about 1.75m high. The carvings on the Battle Stone can be hard to read given that it has been exposed to the elements for a thousand years, but you might be able to discern a Celtic cross, animals, and a horseman. As part of the kirk's plans to make the graveyard more accessible, a metalwork gate has been installed which incorporates the Battle Stone in its design.

Inside the kirk is a 7th century Pictish stone with a carving of the Pictish Beast - an unusual creature, possibly an elephant - the beast is often found on Pictish stones and brooches. The church is locked outside of service hours, but if you are able to gain entry you will also find a medieval knight's tomb.

Dufftown is home to two castles, Balvenie and Auchindoun. **Balvenie Castle** (AB55 4GH ⦿historicenvironment.scot) is less than a mile north from the centre of town. The original castle was built in the late 13th century, making it one of Scotland's oldest stone castles. Over the years it changed hands between the powerful dynasties of the Comyns, and the Black Douglases – and then to the Stewarts who transformed the medieval fortification into an attractive Renaissance residence over the course of 250 years, whilst only paying a single red rose as rent.

Balvenie can only be visited from April 1 to September 30. It is open daily from 9.30am to 5pm but closes for an hour at 12.30 pm. Adult entry is £6, and the site it not accessible for wheelchair users.

High on a hill two miles southeast of Dufftown, the dramatic ruins of 15th-century **Auchindoun Castle** are free to visit and open year round (AB55 4DR ⦿historicenvironment.scot). Follow the A941 south and east out of Dufftown then take the right-hand turning which is signposted for Cabrach and Rhynie to stay on the A941. After a mile you should see a brown tourist sign on the other side of the road, pointing to a rough farm track. At the top of the track there is a small car park. Just beyond the car park a trail to the right will lead you past some trees then over a couple of fields to the castle and some beautiful views. The history of Auchindoun's bloody past is told on interpretation boards located at the site.

Having ventured this far along the A491, you may wish to continue exploring deeper into the outstanding beauty and wilderness of the region known as The Cabrach. A further half-dozen or so miles southeast on the A491 will take you to the Grouse Inn (AB54 4EL ☏01466 702200). A well-respected local inn with a warm welcome, hearty home cooking, and a selection of over 200 whiskies, the Grouse Inn is open from Easter until the end of October.

Glenfiddich Distillery (🖵glenfiddich.com) is located right next to Balvenie Castle. There are many distilleries in Moray which are open to visitors (some only by appointment), and they all have a different tale to tell about the architecture, the history, modernity, and production of whisky. Despite the presence of drinks giants Diageo and Pernod Ricard who own nearly 60% of Moray's distilleries, Glenfiddich remains a family owned and operated distillery since opening in 1887.

The low stone buildings of the distillery are set in beautiful gardens with well-tended flower beds. There is even a pond, the water from which is used for cooling during the distillation process. Small, personally guided tours allow you to explore the stills, warehouses, and bottling hall – culminating in a tutored tasting of three different aged drams, with miniature tasting packs for the

---

Fairy Walk 1.7 miles (7.2km) 1h

Children love discovering Dufftown's magical Fairy Village. Each summer, gorgeous fairy houses magically appear in the woods south of the town. The nearest parking is an area of hard-standing just in front of a few houses that sit on the edge of Mortlach Kirk graveyard. At the bottom of the parking area. Take the footbridge over Dullan Water then right, following the path by the river.

On this walk you will pass the rocky cliff formations of the Giant's Chair, and the hollow Giant's Cradle. When the burn is in full spate you will also see the Linen Apron waterfall – good footwear is recommended.

After discovering the Fairy Village and enjoying some time there, you can either return the way you came, or continue on the path. The trail will join a narrow minor road – turn right and follow it all the way back to the kirk. There is no footpath here so do take care.

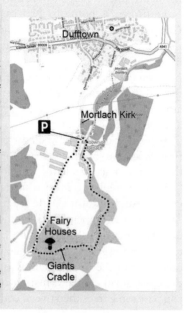

designated driver, all for £20. Breakfast, lunch, and tea & cake are available in the Whisky Lounge from 9.30am to 4pm, with drams served from 11am.

The **Whisky Museum** (10 Conval Street, ⬯whisky.dufftown.co.uk) is staffed by friendly volunteers who are happy to provide lots of information about distillery tours as well as other local attractions and self-guided walks. The specialist museum is full of curiosities related to the whisky industry, including its illegal smuggling history, and the staff love to share stories with visitors. On Wednesday nights in the summer, join them for a whisky nosing at the Royal British Legion: £20 will see you enjoy an evening sampling five Speyside drams, and a keep-sake complimentary Glencairn nosing glass.

Just a minute's walk from the Whisky Museum, is the **Whisky Shop** (1 Fife Street ⬯whiskyshopdufftown.com). This little gem is packed with over 600 whiskies from all over the world, and Mike and Vicky are on hand to help you decide which one is right for you. If you can't decide on one, create your own pick 'n' mix from the vast selection of about a hundred miniatures.

There are lots of beautiful walks in and around Dufftown, and the locally produced booklet 'Paths Around Dufftown,' is available as a PDF (⬯dufftown.co.uk) so you can plan your trip ahead of time. There are fourteen walks in the guide which is peppered with historic notes. The walks vary in duration, and the guide makes it clear how fit and able you need to be to complete each one. Hopefully you will get to see some of the wildlife in the area which includes buzzards, deer, and water vole. If these creatures prove elusive, it is just as thrilling to encounter the majestic, shaggy Highland cattle which are often in the fields near Balvenie Castle.

A couple of the walks will take you past Dufftown Golf Club which has two holes worthy of mention. At 1,294ft above sea level, the ninth tee is Scotland's highest; and the tenth hole 'Glenfiddich,' has the biggest tee-to-green drop in Britain, measuring 339ft (103m).

Dufftown is the first and last destination on the UK's most northerly heritage railway line: **Keith & Dufftown Railway** (⬯keith-dufftown-railway.co.uk). Operating over weekends in the summer months, the first train departs at 10.30am for a forty minute scenic ride through beautiful whisky country to Keith. Following a short lay-over of ten to twenty minutes, the train makes its return journey, but as there are three return trips scheduled, there is plenty of time to disembark and explore the charms of Keith.

The station at Dufftown is a mile walk from the clock tower, up Balvenie Street and mid-way between Glenfiddich and Balvenie distilleries. The ticket hall at the station is delightfully presented in a vintage style with a traditional ticket booth, bunting, and battered old suitcases. The Sidings Café is situated inside a couple of repurposed old carriages on the sidings and offers extremely good value on light lunches and mouth-watering home-bakes. One of the more unusual items on the menu is whisky ice cream. Made in Dufftown, *Balvenie Street*'s Luxury Whisky Ice Cream (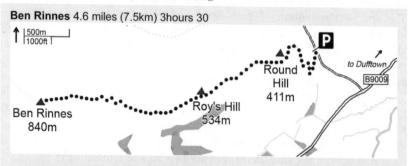whiskyicecream.co.uk) is available in three single malt flavours at Sidings. If you want to try some more, pop into their ice cream shop at 8 Balvenie Street where you can choose from their 'Cask of Characters' prize-winning ice cream range.

Ben Rinnes 4.6 miles (7.5km) 3hours 30

Ben Rinnes is the biggest hill in Moray. At 2,733ft (841m) it falls short of the 3,000ft required to be a Munro, and instead is classified as a Corbett. To access the main route up the Ben, follow the B9009 road south from Dufftown for six and a half miles, then turn right, following the sign to Edinvillie on to an un-named single-track road. The car park is little more than a tarmacked area for five or six cars, just before the access gate to the hill path. There is a layby just after the gate which can be used for additional parking.

If you are coming from Aberlour, leave from the west end of the village. Take care as you will be taking a sharp left up Dowans Road and doubling-back on yourself on a rather fun hair-pin bend. This route is single-track road all the way and has stunning scenery and the dark mass of Ben Rinnes looms ahead of you all the way.

Once parked, head towards the wooden gate where you'll see information here about the Friends of Ben Rinnes and a donation box for funds to assist in the upkeep of the path. Please keep to the path to help limit erosion and protect the Ben.

The walk starts on the other side of the gate, following an inclined track across the left of the hillside. It then zig-zags up to the top of Round Hill and levels out slightly: enjoy the rest and your first view of Ben Rinnes.

The next part is a gentle climb up Roy's Hill, and there is a brief descent before climbing up Black Banks – you are now on the east ridge of Ben Rinnes. The name Black Banks refers to the dark banks of peat which line the side of the path.

The final climb zig-zags up the east ridge of the Ben to the grassy summit which has the rather grand name of Scurran of Lochterlandoch. There are several rocky outcrops here and they can provide a welcome respite from the wind. The trig point is topped with a brass plate which has a 360° map to help identify points on the fabulous views, all the way from the blue waters of the Moray Firth to the dark mountains of the Cairngorms.

The summit is home to a colony of shy ptarmigan. These beautiful little grouse live on the top of mountains and change their speckled brown summer plumage to a brilliant white in winter.

In 2022, the **Dufftown Highland Games** (◉dufftownhighlandgames.com) celebrates 130 years of pageantry. Held on the last Saturday in July, competitions begin at 10.30am with Highland dancing, and continue throughout the day with traditional heavy-weight challenges including the caber toss. The Massed Bands Parade sees hundreds of pipers from upwards of ten different pipe bands receive permission from Chieftain Alex Grant to march from the iconic Dufftown Clock Tower to the games during the opening ceremony. Thousands of visitors come to enjoy a day of dance music and athletics - for the overseas visitors, there is the opportunity to take part in a special race.

As well as heading up the massed pipe bands, Dufftown & District Pipe Band play in the square twice a month during July and August. On New Year's Day they accompany a very special parade of Dufftown Juvenile Society. Started in 1835 as a method of collecting tools for apprentices, the annual Boys Parade sees girls and boys, waving toy swords and flags, leading a procession through the town to raise money for local charities and organisations.

One of the more extreme events at Dufftown Highland Games is the Ben Rinnes 5 Tops Hill Race. This race is for experienced runners only and requires that participants carry full body waterproofs, a map, compass, whistle, and emergency food over a fourteen mile course. Setting off at midday, competitors pass the summits of Little Conval and Meikle Conval en route to Ben Rinnes, and return by the same path, climbing a total of 5,000ft over the length of the course.

CRAIGELLACHIE

The pretty little terraced village of Craigellachie is located on high ground, above the confluence of the Fiddich and Spey whisky rivers, looking towards the forested hill on the far side of the Spey.

There are two Craigellachies, the other being a high hill which overlooks Aviemore, and in the halcyon days of the clan system, the land between these two points, was the country of the Grants. 'Stand fast, Craigellachie!' being the cry of the clansmen.

The Grants spread further downstream and are linked with at least ten distilleries in the area, including Glen Grant, the best-selling whisky in Italy, which was established by brothers James and John Grant in 1840, and William Grant & Sons who established Glenfiddich (1887), and Balvenie (1892).

There has been a settlement at Craigellachie since 1750, when records indicate that there was a ferry crossing to Boat of Fiddich. As the local whisky industry boomed, the railway came to Speyside in the 1860s, and a viaduct was constructed across the Spey to carry the trains which would serve the numerous distilleries in the area. The railway operated for over a hundred years, but no part of the original Strathspey Railway exists, just the connections at either end to the heritage lines at Aviemore, and Dufftown. The Strathspey Railway route now forms part of the Speyside Way from Ballindalloch to Spey Bay, and walkers pass through the atmospheric Craigellachie Tunnel when they journey between Craigellachie and Aberlour.

Craigellachie is a popular over-night stop for those on the long distance route, and the start/stop point is at Fiddich Park in the northeast corner of the village. Walkers will most likely want to stop at the welcoming site of **The Fiddichside Inn** (📞07841 357637 🌐fiddichside.com) for a celebratory dram, and anglers can sit and share tales of the one that got away.

The picturesque Fiddichside Inn, which has long been a favourite spot with locals and international tourists, was owned and managed by local legend Joe Smith until his passing in 2017. Originally built as 'refreshment rooms' for the railway, the cosy riverside pub is now owned by Ali Hunter and her son Guy. In-line with Joe's legacy, the pub continues to offer good old-fashioned hospitality with a beautiful beer garden right on the bank of the River Fiddich, whilst the attached cottage is now available as a holiday let.

Marvel at the skilled craftsmen making whisky barrels in the Speyside Cooperage.

For a small village, Craigellachie has a good range of accommodation to choose from, whatever type of catering you prefer: B&B, a luxury Victorian lodge, and two hotels which boast award-winning whisky bars.

The Highlander Inn (10 Victoria Street 📞01340 881446 🌐whiskyinn.com) offers 8 en-suite bedrooms with more off-site, and a menu of hearty pub-classics. It's a no-frills traditional bar, popular with locals, with a large, sunny patio, friendly staff, and more than 400 whiskies, including the largest selection of Japanese whiskies available outside of Southeast Asia.

The **Copper Dog** is the name of the pub at the **Craigellachie Hotel** (Victoria Street 📞01340 881204 🌐craigellachiehotel.co.uk) – it is also the name of the hotel's very own whisky, blended from eight single malts. Designed by Charles Doig (architect of the iconic vents on many distilleries) and built in 1893 as the 'Craigellachie Railway Hotel', it has 26 rooms and was once rented out by super-model Kate Moss for a star-studded party. With live music every Friday and Saturday night, the Copper Dog pub is at the heart of the hotel, busy with guests as well as locals popping in for a pint and a pub meal. It's the Quaich Bar however, which is outstanding.

Founded in 1893, The Quaich is the world's leading whisky bar and features over 900 single malt whiskies. It's not just the quantity of drams, but the quality: the menu features many unique and rare whiskies, all available by the glass.

Whether you drink your whisky neat, on the rocks, or in a classic cocktail, at the Quaich you will be enjoying it in beautiful surroundings which feature elegant, hand-crafted furniture, and a bar which is lined with a band of silver.

From the front of the Craigellachie Hotel, one can see the beautiful **Craigellachie Bridge**, also known as the Telford Bridge. By 1812, the ferry service across the Spey was proving insufficient and unreliable – frequently disrupted for days when the river was too dangerous to cross – and so engineer Thomas Telford was commissioned to build a bridge. Now the oldest cast-iron bridge in Scotland, the Telford Bridge is a graceful single-span of ironwork with a pair of castellated turrets on either side of the road. From a distance it appears as though the west side of the bridge is built into the very cliff face. There is in fact a sharp right turn, which wasn't problematic for pedestrians or cattle-drives, but did make it unsuitable for modern vehicles and a replacement road bridge was built in 1970.

Access is on foot, through the playing field across the road from the Craigellachie Hotel. Take the tarmacked access road down towards a parking area. Beyond the car park, you will find safe passage under the busy road. Either follow the path all the way round to first enjoy views from the edge of the River Spey or take the left-hand path once under the A491 to go straight to the bridge at road level.

Once across Craigellachie Bridge, it's only a two mile walk to The Macallan Distillery and Visitor Centre. The Macallan have built a state of the art production facility, much of which is hidden underground and is bursting with technological innovations. There's also a stylish bar and brasserie, all discretely contained within a piece of modern, organic architecture which emulates the rolling hills of the surrounding countryside, and still located on the doorstep of iconic Easter Elchies House – the spiritual home of The Macallan, a likeness of which adorns all their bottles. Visitors can book tours of the distillery, tastings, and dining experiences on Saturday and Sunday, and explore the grounds of Easter Elchies House. Access to the house is available on select distillery tours (page 23).

There are two distilleries associated with Craigellachie, and the second, John Dewar & Sons, is located right in the village, on Hill Street. Dewars blend the aged Craigellachie single malt and offer a tantalising glimpse at the pot stills through their large windows, They only open their doors to the lucky few who are visiting the springtime Spirit of Speyside Festival.

Continue east along Hill Street to the edge of the village and the **Speyside Cooperage** (Dufftown Road &01340 871108 speysidecooperage.co.uk). An integral part of the whisky industry, coopers build and repair the oak casks which are central to developing the subtle whisky aromas. A busy, five-star tourist attraction (and part of the Malt Whisky Trail), the Speyside Cooperage is the only cooperage in Britain with a visitor centre. Book a spot on one of their hourly tours (£4) which start with an excellent augmented audio-visual presentation, followed by the opportunity to find out about the lifecycle of a cask and watch the incredibly skilled coopers hard at work from the viewing gallery. You will be accompanied by a friendly guide who can answer all your questions.

No tour would be complete without a visit to the gift shop which has a diverse range of artisan products created from barrels and staves, as well as beautiful jewellery, and luxury Scottish products – the gift shop is the only place in the world you can buy the bespoke Speyside Cooperage single malt. After your tour, take a short drive around the corner and have a peak in the yard where up to 200,000 barrels are stacked in impressive oak pyramids.

BALLINDALLOCH ESTATE

The Ballindalloch Estate stretches from the Glenlivet Estate in the south, to Glenfarclas in the north. Ballindalloch itself is a small village within the estate, and it was served by a railway station for 100 years from 1863. The station had special structures to deal with the whisky industry including a siding which went straight to Cragganmore Distillery, and a two-storey building constructed especially for whisky storage. Cragganmore was co-founded in 1869, between Sir George Macpherson-Grant, the 3rd Baronet of Ballindalloch, and John Smith of The Glenlivet.

Ballindalloch Castle (℡01807 500205 ballindallochcastle.co.uk) is known as the Pearl of the North and has been home to the Macpherson-Grant family since 1546. A beautiful baronial castle, it started life as a traditional fortress and over the centuries was transformed into the turreted residence you see today. Visitors are welcome at the castle and can explore some of the grand rooms where collections of weaponry and china are on display.

As you drive up the long private access road to the castle, look out for the first clump of trees before a right-hand bend. Within these trees are the Marionburgh Stones, the remains of a circular cairn about 45ft (14m) in diameter which date from about 2000BC. Nine stones remain in this group, and of them, five are standing, two have fallen, one is leaning, and one is in a wall.

Romantic Ballindalloch Castle is set in beautiful gardens. Enjoy a stroll by the banks of the rivers Spey and Avon.

The gardens of the castle have been designed to delight year round. Planned in three sections, visitors can explore the Rockery which climbs the lower slopes of the valley; enjoy the classical Courtyard Garden; or head down the tree-lined avenue to the Walled Garden where careful planting ensures colour and perfume in every season. Beautifully illustrated maps of walks around the gardens and estate are available at the castle and online.

After your tour of the castle and gardens, be sure to see if anything takes your eye in the giftshop which is stocked with items including luxury accessories and locally made produce. Of course, no castle visit is complete without a stop in the tearoom, where you can enjoy a simple, hearty soup and a sandwich, or tuck into delicious cake made on the premises.

Last stop on your visit at Ballindalloch Castle might be the bathroom facilities which won 'Best Loos' at the Hudson's Heritage Awards.

In 2011, the idea of **Ballindalloch Distillery** (&01807 500331 ballindallochdistillery.com) was conceived. In today's society where it is important to leave as small a footprint as possible, the single estate whisky takes barley grown on Ballindalloch Home Farm to make the spirit and returns the waste products as feed for Ballindalloch's prize-winning Aberdeen Angus cattle, and fertiliser for the fields. On the far side of the River Avon, and just over a mile's walk from the Castle, the distillery is set on the old farm steading at Lagmore, and visitors are welcome to take a tour.

The Ballindalloch Estate is home to over a hundred cattle, from the oldest herd of Aberdeen Angus in the world. Instantly recognisable by their glossy black hides, the bloodline of these Aberdeen Angus can be traced back to 1860.

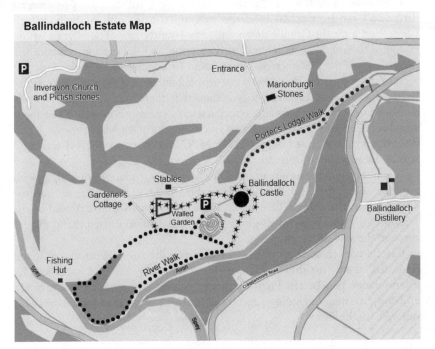

Ballindalloch Estate Map

Fellow enthusiasts of these magnificent animals can arrange a farm visit to indulge their passion.

As well as grazing pastures for these pedigree cows, the estate is comprised of forests, moors, and arable farms. Much of the crop grown is Laureate barley, which is used in the following year's whisky production. Across Moray trees are an important crop, and commercial forestry is carefully managed to help maintain a balance between industry and habitat for animals including the local resident deer population, and rarer creatures including pine martens and wildcats.

Sensitive land management of a diverse range of habitats, alongside the conservation work of the ghillies and gamekeepers of the estate, has resulted in healthy populations of indigenous wildlife. Black grouse, golden plovers, curlews and capercaillie thrive on the moors; and both red deer, and roe deer can be found in the woodlands. The estate has two salmon rivers running through it, the Spey and the Avon. Anglers come from all over the world to fish for these magnificent creatures on a catch and release basis – applications are welcome from keen fishermen.

Nestled in the heart of the estate is an 18-hole (9 green) golf course. Designed by Donald Steer, the course is open to visitors.

Inveravon Church (sometimes written as 'Inveraven', pronounced 'Inveraan') can be reached by car, a mile-and-a-half north of Ballindalloch Castle, and a third of a mile down a narrow country lane. The interior of the church is as simple as its white-harled exterior, and the grounds contain the mausoleum of the Macpherson-Grant family of Ballindalloch Castle.

Whilst it is possible that there was a chapel built here in the early 6th century by the Pictish saint Drostan, it is certain that there was a church in 1108, dedicated to St Peter who is also associated with a nearby holy well. The church stood for nearly seven hundred years, and during the re-building process, it was discovered that at least one of the Pictish stones (now on display) was used within the structure of the early church.

When the church was rebuilt in 1806 as a modest, rectangular building, with a simple belfry, four Pictish stones from the 6th-8th century were set into the south wall of the church. Over the centuries, the stones were exposed to the freeze-thaw cycle of Scottish winters, and their location caused damp ingress through the wall of the church.

Careful conservation work in 2011 removed the stones from the wall and relocated them to the north porch where they are accompanied by interpretation panels. The Pictish-style carvings on the stones include animals, and domestic items including a comb and mirror. The north porch is open daily during daylight hours.

ABERLOUR

Speyside Way Visitor Centre (seasonal) Broomfield Square 📞01340 881724
🖰 speysidevisitorcentre.scot

Charlestown of Aberlour, the main village within the parish of Aberlour, is simply referred to as 'Aberlour,' by locals. Charles Grant, 2nd Laird of West Elchies founded the village in 1812, selling 100 plots of land to local crofters under the feu system. The main street runs parallel to the River Spey, and behind the village a short walk will take you to the beautiful Falls of Linn of Ruthrie, generally known as Linn Falls.

The northern approach to the village takes you through some beautiful deciduous woodland with frequent glimpses of the River Spey to the west. Aberlour is the home of **Walkers Shortbread** (Fisherton Industrial Estate, 📞01340 871 555 🖰walkershortbread.com), and their factory is the first building you will see when you arrive from the north. From its humble beginnings in 1898 when Joseph Walker borrowed £50 to open a village bakery, Walkers is now Scotland's biggest exporter of food and has been awarded Royal

Highland Games by the Spey, Walker's shortbread, and a picturesque waterfall.

Warrants for supplies of shortbread and oatcakes. The firm is run by Joseph's grandchildren and great-grandchildren, and all new recipes are tested by the lucky residents of Aberlour – Joseph Walker's bakery is still trading at 99 High Street. There are no tours of the factory, but there is a shortbread shop within the factory grounds where you can load up on baked goods and merchandise bearing Walkers' iconic red and black tartan livery. Grab a bargain and get your hands on some broken biscuits: they taste just as good as the perfectly packaged ones which make their way to the shelves of fine food stores around the world.

The headquarters for Walkers are in Aberlour House. This stunning country house was built in 1838 for William Grant who made his fortune as a plantation owner and sugar merchant in Jamaica. Upon Grant's death, the estate passed to his niece Margaret Macpherson Grant who used her inheritance to benefit the local community. Margaret founded Aberlour Orphanage in 1875 and commissioned St Margaret's Episcopal Church to serve it. Although Margaret died just two years later, aged 42, her work at the Orphanage was continued by Canon Charles Jupp whom she appointed as Administrator. St Margaret's Church was completed with funding from William Grant, nephew of the founder of Aberlour. With a wing each for boys and girls, and a school, Aberlour Orphanage grew to become the second largest children's home, housing up to two hundred orphans at its peak, and some 6,000 children from across Britain over its lifetime.

The pretty church of **St Margaret's** (☎01340 871529 ⌨stmargaretsaberlour.co.uk) stands at the north end of Aberlour and is set far back from the main road, at the end of a field which may have a couple of horses in it. Access is via a tree-lined drive, just before Mitre Cottage (1 High Street) and signs on the wrought iron railings welcome you to visit. Inside the church, polished pillars of pink granite topped with intricate stonework support the arches of the side-aisles. Light filters down through the windows which contain beautiful stained glass depictions of the saints and biblical stories. Beneath your feet the central passage of the nave is covered in decorative tiling whilst the flooring of the chancel has even more beautiful mosaics.

The church is locked outside of service hours, but a key is available from the Aberlour Hotel (87 High Street ☎01340 871287 ⌨aberlourhotel.co.uk) should you wish to look around the building.

The orphanage ceased operating in 1967 and the orphanage buildings have been demolished, leaving only the clock tower and a memorial garden at the top of Conval Drive. A footpath leads from the church, through a wooden gate, joining with Conval Drive – or return to High Street and turn left just two blocks south of the access road for St Margaret's Church.

Like many planned villages in Moray, Aberlour has broad streets and a central square. Occupying a sunny spot, the leafy square is enclosed by green hedges and criss-crossed by diagonal paths in a St Andrew's cross, whilst flowerbeds of roses and colourful planters add to its charm. The village's war memorial is here: erected in 1921, it was designed to look like an ancient market cross.

Many of the village shops are concentrated in this area, and you are spoiled for choice when it comes to dining. Up and down High Street there is a range of cafés and hotels, providing options which range from freshly made sandwiches to three-course luxury dining experiences. The **Speyside Larder** (96/98 High Street) will see you sorted for an amazing picnic. The walls of the delicatessen are lined with dark wood shelves giving the store a distinctly vintage feel. Well-stocked with the impressive selection of whiskies that you come to expect in this part of the world, the shelves are also full of fine wines and even some Scottish mead. Their fridges are packed with locally produced, award-winning pies and cakes, marinated olives, international cheeses, and charcuterie. Pair a decadent pear & partridge pâté with some delicious oatcakes and pop a locally brewed ale into your backpack before heading off on an adventure.

Inside a popular café called **The Gather'n**, is **3 Bags Wool** (89 High Street). This craft shop sells thrums, a by-product from the Scottish weaving industry. 'Thrum', is a Scottish word which describes the ends of warp threads left attached to the loom and at 3 Bags Wool you can buy these fabric strips in a gorgeous array of colours and designs, which you can then knit or crochet with their specially designed needles and hooks.

At **The Gallery in Aberlour and Spey Sport** (79 High Street) you are as likely to find a handsome tweed ghillies cap and some necessary fishing tackle, as you are a beautiful piece of locally created art and some luxury homeware.

Behind the square is **Aberlour Parish Church**. It was built in 1812 to replace an older church which was located a short distance to the west, and in 1840 the tower was added. The parish church suffered a significant fire in 1861: only the tower remained, and the nave had to be rebuilt. In the 21st century, the interior was renovated, and the result is a modern space with a nod to its past by the retention of some 1930s pews and a small pipe organ believed to be from the same decade.

The railway used to run past Aberlour, and if you walk from the parish church tower, west towards the Spey, you will come to the old railway station. The original building houses the Speyside Visitor Centre and was extended in 2004 to include the **Speyside Way Visitor Centre** (Broomfield Square ☎01340 881724 📱speysidevisitorcentre.scot). Open seasonally, the staff here can help you with everything from maps for local walks, to information about wildlife, attractions and transport, and finding accommodation. Housed within the Visitor Centre, the Old Station Tea Room is very popular for anyone in need of refreshments and splendid home-bakes.

The **Mash Tun** (8 Broomfield Square ☎01340 881771 📱mashtun-aberlour.com) is a stone's throw from the Visitor Centre and used to be The Station Bar. Built in 1896 by James Campbell, it has a uniquely rounded gable due to the fact that Campbell was a sea captain, and he had instructed a marine architect to design the building in the shape of a small ship.

The beautiful expanse of parkland between the Mash Tun and the River Spey is Alice Littler Memorial Park. The paths around the park run from up past the Speyside Visitor Centre, down to the Victoria Bridge, an attractive suspension footbridge built about 1900. Prior to the construction of the bridge, the only way across the fast-flowing river to Elchies was by ferry boat. James Fleming, owner of Aberlour Distillery, bequeathed £500 for the construction of a bridge to provide safe passage over the Spey. Initially, the Laird of Elchies, William Grant, refused permission for the bridge to be sited on his side of the river, but after being presented with a letter reminding him about recent loss of life when a ferry boat capsized, Grant eventually gave permission for the bridge, and oversaw the construction. He also erected a gate on his own side of the bridge, charging a toll of one penny to cross.

Each year, on the first Saturday in August, the **Aberlour Strathspey Highland Games** (☎07771 773859 📱aberlourhighlandgames.co.uk ⏱11am-6pm) take place in the park on the banks of the River Spey. A relative newcomer to the scene, Aberlour Games were first held in 1943 and now attract over 5,000 spectators from all over the world. Recently awarded runner-up for the best sporting event in Scotland, the Aberlour Games deliver a high calibre of competition and entertainment.

Competitions start at 11am with traditional Highland dancing and continue throughout the day. One of the highlights of the event is undoubtedly the parade of the massed pipe bands, as the assembled drummers and pipers in full tartan regalia march through the village and down into the park for 1pm, when Chieftain Guy Macpherson-Grant of Ballindalloch Castle officially declares the games underway. The afternoon continues with traditional events, (including caber-tossing), and overseas visitors are encouraged to have a go at haggis hurlin' and tug o' war.

Spectators are well catered for with a beer tent and food stalls, whilst shoppers are bound to find something that takes their fancy at one of the many trade and craft stands. The events draw to a close at 6pm as the massed pipe bands march down the main street of Aberlour and perform a spine-tingling set in the village square.

At the most southerly end of Aberlour High Street the current village cemetery backs on to the old parish graveyard. The most obvious structure in the graveyard is the gothic mausoleum of the Macpherson-Grants of Aberlour House, built in 1859. The mausoleum was built next to the remains of the old parish church of St Drostan. It is possible that St Drostan founded a monastery here in 618AD, and there are references to a medieval church. Hidden under a growth of ivy which is almost as tall as the mausoleum, are the remains of a wall of the last known church on this site which was in use until the Aberlour Parish Church on Victoria Terrace was constructed. Close by, a large stone font believed to have belonged to the old church has been preserved, mounted on a stone plinth.

Beyond the old graveyard, the Burn of Aberlour flows into the River Spey and near the main road a pretty 17th-century pack bridge crosses the burn. A small hump-backed bridge, the surface of which is now turfed over, it was originally known as the Bridge of Skirdustan (St Drustan/Drostan) the old name of the settlement which predated modern Aberlour, and it has since been re-named as the Bridge of Charlestown.

The Burn of Aberlour, also known as the Lour Burn, flows through the grounds of Aberlour Distillery, the entrance to which is located on the other side of the high street from the pack bridge – just look for the handsome gatehouse. Founded by James Fleming in 1879, **Aberlour Distillery** (✆01340 881249 ⌂maltwhiskydistilleries.com/aberlour) was built on the site of a previous distillery which had been destroyed by fire. Fleming bought the land and built his own distillery. In 1898 another fire destroyed all bar one of the distillery buildings, and new buildings were constructed featuring the Charles Doig vent. The source of the water for Aberlour's whisky expressions come from a spring associated with baptisms performed by St Drostan, whilst water from the Lour is used in the cooling process. Visitors over the age of 18 are welcome at the distillery, and booking is recommended for the tours which start at £20 for a one hour tour featuring tastings of six expressions.

A short walk from the Aberlour Distillery, are the double-cascades of the **Falls of Linn of Ruthrie**. Referred to locally as the Linn Falls, a circular walk along the Burn of Aberlour will take you behind the distillery to the cool dark pools of the waterfall. The area around the falls is a pretty woodland gorge with a mix of deciduous and pine trees, with green ferns adorning the rock face of the falls themselves.

The walk begins on a lane on the other side of the Lour from the Aberlour Distillery Visitor Centre. Follow the burn upstream, passing an abandoned stone cottage on your left, and then the distillery buildings on the far side of the burn, enjoying the sweet smells of the whisky making process as you go. You will come to a grassy area with a view of the pools which makes an ideal picnic spot – you might even see cold-water swimmers braving the plunge below the tumbling waters. Keep on the path up the side of the falls to enjoy the cascades from above.

To continue on the circular walk, follow the route curving left uphill, alongside the handrail. The trail will lead out of the woods and onto a lane that runs between some very pretty gardens. At the end of the gardens, turn left downhill towards Allachie Drive, then right onto Chapel Terrace, and finally onto Queen's Road to arrive back at the square in the centre of the village where you will find cafés and restaurants for some welcome refreshments.

KNOCKANDO

Knockando is a farming community on the west side of the River Spey. It is home to both the Knockando and Tamdhu distilleries, although neither of these offer tours. Instead, Knockando has something different for visitors to experience. At the heart of a lush green valley, the picturesque **Knockando Woolmill** (Aberlour AB38 7RP ☎01340 810345 ⌨kwm.co.uk) has been converting fleeces into fabric and yarn for over 230 years. At one time, small local mills were commonplace in north-east Scotland. Industrialisation fuelled

A wee gem – Knockando Woolmill is a fascinating attraction in a scenic setting .

the large textile industries in the Scottish borders, and as the large mills modernised, some district mills would buy up their second-hand machinery whilst others were dissolved in the face of competition. Many small mills ceased trading between the two world wars, but Knockando Woolmill managed to carry on.

The mill has only changed ownership a few times throughout its history, and although it was handed over to the Knockando Woolmill Trust in the year 2000, it is still very much under the skilled management of Hugh Jones who has worked there since the 1970s.

The mill and its Victorian machinery were listed by Historic Scotland as being of international importance, but both the buildings and their contents were in need of a lot of attention. The Trust raised £3.5 million to transform the rusted iron roof, wooden flooring, and damaged masonry, as well as repair the worn machinery. The result is very sympathetic to the formerly dilapidated buildings: the unique window frames which are incorporated in the mill's own tartan have been restored and even the old water wheel has been refurbished with the intention of it providing power to the mill again.

Today, the mill specialises in small batch yarns and fabrics for luxury markets, including a new hardwearing tweed for the family and staff of Logie Estate near Forres, and a new stylish tweed for Edinburgh Castle.

Knockando Woolmill is located just half a mile away from the Speyside Way – midway through the Craigellachie to Ballindalloch section it makes a perfect breakpoint for walkers and cyclists. Visitors to the mill might find themselves lucky enough to experience the machinery in action, from the soft whispers of the teasing and carding processes to the clatter of the loom and shuttle.

The Trust have put a lot of effort into creating an excellent visitor experience. Entry is free, and the working mill and visitor centre contain interpretation boards and videos to help you get the most from your visit. The first building is the beautifully restored old shop which features examples of fine plaids and tweeds, a hand-operated machine used in stitching blankets, and an old wooden till. Inside the cottage there are lots of interesting exhibits. The entrance hallway retains its original wallpaper, preserved behind perspex sheets. About 40 wallpapers were found in the cottage and they make for a fascinating piece of history – some have been displayed as samples in an album whilst others remain in situ. Take a seat in the parlour where a short film explains the heritage of the mill, and shows the incredible skills required to work the different machinery. The exhibition continues in the kitchen which features an old black range and a spinning wheel. Information boards, photographs, and elements from the industry illustrate over two hundred years of woollen manufacture.

The long white building which houses the main machinery of the mill is also open to visitors. The heavy Victorian machinery isn't usually in operation, but it is easy to imagine the great noise from the variety of machines which are part of the process from carding to spinning and weaving.

The gift shop sells wool and fabric from the mill, both of which are available in their basic state for you to create your own clothing, or already transformed into stylish accessories including scarves and notebooks. The mill is set in beautiful gardens which have been landscaped by the BBC's Beechgrove Garden team and are a delight to explore. Before you leave, take a wander down by the Knockando Burn which once powered the mill.

GLENLIVET ESTATE

From the early 1500s **Glenlivet Estate** (🌐glenlivetestate.co.uk) was the property of the Gordon family, until 1937 when it was acquired by the Crown Estate Scotland. At 656ft (200m) above sea-level, and flanked by the Cromdale Hills on the northwest, and the Ladder Hills on the southwest, Glenlivet Estate is almost 57,000 acres of fertile land populated by villages, farms, and commercial forests.

When the Duke of Gordon established Tomintoul on his estate, he encouraged the production of linen as a means of supporting the village. The industry wasn't a success locally, and instead people were dependent on raising cattle and crops. In 1788, stills producing less than 99 gallons (450lt) were outlawed, and a report in 1797 indicated there were 37 families in the village, 'without any industry. All of them sell whisky, and all of them drink it'.

The Excise Act of 1823 allowed the making of whisky under licence, and one of the first people to take advantage of this was George Smith. Transferring his illegal trade to licenced production, Smith became the first legal distiller in the parish of Glenlivet, producing the world-famous whisky, The Glenlivet.

Sporting opportunities range from traditional salmon fishing and deer stalking to more modern pursuits including a dedicated mountain bike centre. The red trail offers some of the longest downhill mountain biking in the UK.

Careful management of the Estate has resulted in several special habitats for wildlife. As well as red squirrels and red deer, Glenlivet is also home to rare species including black grouse and golden eagles, wildcats, and pine martens.

The estate provides detailed maps with plotted walks, parking and picnic areas, viewpoints, and places of interest. Guided walks with a Glenlivet Estate ranger are organised as fun family events. In autumn, join a special ranger-led walk along the River Livet for the chance to experience the red deer rut.

For something a bit different, try an award-winning tour with Glenlivet Hill Trek (📞01807 590372 🌐glenlivethilltrek.com). Full day Land Rover tours, and half day guided treks include distillery visits, smuggler's tales, and exclusive historical sites.

Tomintoul makes a good base to start exploring Glenlivet from. The Glenlivet Estate Visitor Centre is at the south end of the village and there is free parking even when the centre is closed. The Glenlivet Estate website is a great resource for walks in the area, including Scalan Seminary, and smugglers trails – you can download a beautifully designed map from the 'walking' section of their website.

To the northwest of Tomintoul you will find the twin arched structure of the Avon Bridge. Both the Avon Bridge and the Old Bridge of Livet (a packhorse bridge the north of the estate), are beautiful structures and provide a great place to enjoy a picnic and take some photographs.

Built at the foot of the Cromdale Hills in 1964, **Tomintoul Distillery** (AB37 9AQ &01807 590274 Ⓞtomintoulwhisky.com) is home to the world's largest bottle of whisky. The bottle is on display in their visitor centre.

Alternatively, head southeast to the Well of Lecht car park and enjoy a walk to the old crushing mill building of the **Lecht Mine**, where information boards at the abandoned mine explain the local mining history.

Drumin Castle in the north of the estate is a ruined 14th century tower house. Use the nearby car park and stretch your legs on a winding walk up to the ruins for fabulous views.

Also located in the north of the estate is **The Glenlivet Distillery** (AB37 9DB &01340 821720 Ⓞmaltwhiskydistilleries.com/theglenlivet). Open seasonally, the recently renewed visitor centre welcomes guests to enjoy hosted tasting experiences in the multi-sensory Provenance Room. Walk through stylised fields of waving barley and meet some of the people who have helped make The Glenlivet what it is today. The bar is modern, luxurious, and yet cosy at the same time with different themed areas where you can enjoy a dram. Two-hundred years of history have been distilled into an award-winning visitor experience and exclusive expressions are available for purchase in the gift shop where you can create a bespoke label and even fill your own bottle from a cask.

Leave your car at the distillery and enjoy a short walk to Blairfindy Castle. Built in 1564, the castle was burned by troops after the Battle of Culloden and never repaired. Recent work to stabilise the remaining structure means that the castle is now accessible to the public.

By day, Blairfindy Moor is an expanse of heathery moorland which makes up part of the Speyside Way spur path linking Ballindalloch with Tomintoul and Glenlivet. It offers stunning scenic views of Ben Rinnes and the Cromdale Hills. By night, it is a recommended **Dark Sky Discovery Site** where low levels of light pollution provide dramatic stargazing opportunities for the aurora borealis, meteor showers and gazing at our amazing galaxy.

TOMINTOUL

Tomintoul Museum and Visitor Information Centre (seasonal) The Square &01807 580760 Ⓞtgdt.org.uk ⨍TomintoulDiscoveryCentre

At 1,164ft (350m), Tomintoul is the highest village in Moray. Located on the eastern edge the Cairngorms National Park, this pretty village is a fine example of 18th-century civic planning: the main street is 40ft (12.2m) wide, and there is a central square with many Georgian and Victorian buildings. There is an excellent selection of pubs, hotels and restaurants for dining, and some charming shops. Situated on the south-western edge of the Glenlivet Estate, Tomintoul is a popular stop with cyclist and walkers exploring the trails.

Prior to the construction of Tomintoul in 1775, there had been settlements in the area since the 1640s, and cattle rustling, and illicit whisky production were very much a way of life for local people. The Duke of Gordon was instrumental in the planning of the village: he had hopes of improving the miserable lives of remote crofters, whilst clamping down on the illegal activities at the same time.

The location of Tomintoul takes advantage of an old military road. The year 1745 saw the final failure of the Jacobite rebellion – a series of attempts which commenced in 1689 by Catholic James Stuart (father of Bonnie Prince Charlie) to *Discover the remoteness of Scalan Seminary, and the beauty of the stars in the night sky.* take the crown from a succession of Protestant monarchs, culminating in the Battle of Culloden.

In 1715, the British Government started building a series of military roads in Scotland as a response to the uprising, and as part of an attempt to bring order to rebellious regions. Construction of the Braemar to Inverness section, via the Lecht pass at Tomintoul, did not begin until 1753, and was the last of the major military roads to be built. A marker stone near the Lecht Mine car park commemorates the men who built the roads. The **Lecht Mine** (AB37 9ES) was the largest manganese mine in Scotland. When it opened in the 1730s, it was mined for iron ore which was smelted in Nethy Bridge; and in the 1840s it supplied manganese which was shipped to Newcastle for use in the manufacture of household bleach.

In the 1700s Catholicism was prohibited, yet in the hills near Tomintoul, a secret seminary was established at **Scalan** (🖥scalan.co.uk ⏲daily), and here is where young priests were trained. Over one hundred priests had been trained here by 1799 when Scalan reverted to a farm. It eventually fell into disuse but has recently been turned into a museum which is open year round. The hidden nature of the seminary means that the museum is not easy to get to, but it can be reached by walking half a mile along a rough country track from the Carrachs car park.

The Carrachs car park is one of the recommended **Dark Sky Discovery Sites** for stargazing in the Cairngorms and Scalan is signposted on the B9008 as you head south from Tomnavoulin to Auchnarrow. Follow the single-track tarmacked road for just over three miles, heading deeper into the countryside until you reach the parking area – there is an information board here with some stargazing facts.

Set out on foot along a farm road – at the start of the walk, there is a pine plantation on your right, and seasonal flowers including purple march orchids populate your route. Along the path a series of plaques on wooden plinths illustrated with photos from the late 1800s give insights into what life was like for people living and working in these remote places. It's a beautiful walk as you head into the Braes of Glenlivet towards the seminary. The trail is strewn with tufts of fleece from wandering sheep, and even in summer pockets of snow can still be seen on the hillside. One can imagine the Heather Priests (as they were known) feeling safe from persecution as they continued their training at the hidden seminary.

A few farm buildings with red wooden doors are the first indicators that you have reached the seminary, and you can see the blue front door of the priests' college peeking through some trees. The old stone mills still have farming machinery and stable furniture in them. The southernmost building recalls the life of Sandy Matheson who was born at Scalan in 1916. Sandy was a tenant at the farm until he retired in 2003, aged 87. Open the doors in the mill and discover evidence of how this crofter and his community would cut peats for the fire and prepare the grain from harvest using the old water-driven threshing machine which is displayed alongside well-worn hand tools.

Inside the seminary, the bare-walled rooms are labelled with descriptions of how they were used in the 1700s, as well as later when the building was re-purposed as a farmhouse. Some of the men of reverence who lectured the trainees are immortalised in reproduced portraits, and the students' timetable illustrates the rigour of their training from 6am to 9pm. The chapel room on the upper floor still contains a simple cross and altar.

The Annual Scalan Mass is held on the first Sunday of July at 4pm in the gardens in front of the seminary. Attended by hundreds of pilgrims, the mass honours the people who risked their lives to keep the Catholic faith alive in times of persecution.

Back on the B9008 at Auchnarrow, continue south towards Tomintoul. Before you have travelled even a quarter of a mile, look out on the right-hand side of the road for a small 'visitors parking' layby. The parking is provided by Heatherhills Fold who advertise their association with **Highland cattle** by a handsome wrought iron sign which features a Highland cow and her calf. The farm specialises in breeding these iconic shaggy beasts and you can often see half-a-dozen or so in the field beside the layby. The breed is native to the western Highlands and although the red-dun colour is what we are most familiar with, the cattle can also be black, yellow, brindle, and even white and silver. Their long wavy, oily outer coats help shake off the rain, and a downy under coat keeps them warm in winter. A long fringe and a broad set of horns complete the classic look for these beautiful animals, and the calves are just adorably fluffy creatures.

Five miles south-east of Tomintoul, along the A939 which follows the route of the old military road, is the **Lecht** ski resort. The Lecht opened in the 1970s, and the fortunes of Tomintoul have been closely tied to it. Whilst the Cairngorms help protect Tomintoul (and Moray) from much rainfall, they also provide snow, and this section of the A939 is regularly the first to be closed in Great Britain due to snowfall.

Head north from Tomintoul, and less than a mile outside of the village you should see a square structure on top of a hill. Pull into the parking area at the disused **Tomintoul Quarry**, and take a short walk to discover *Still*, an art installation created in 2018 by Scottish architects Angus Ritchie and Daniel Tyler. On a high viewpoint, *Still* sits on a base constructed of rocks from the quarry below. Its reflective surfaces create an illusion of infinite dramatic skies and stunning scenery. The installation is one of three works of art which were commissioned to enhance the Snow Road, a 90 mile scenic route which passes through Tomintoul en route from Blairgowrie to Grantown-on-Spey and is a must for a photo-stop and breath-taking views.

Another feature on the Snow Road is the Fodderletter Lum. 'Lum' is a Scots word for chimney, and the Fodderletter Lum is one of a series of isolated stone chimneys which were built by early road menders. These are stand-alone structures – not ruins – and this one is located another mile or so north of *Still*. At the junction for Fodderletter, there is a layby, but no signpost. Pull into the layby and walk the short distance down the joining road to the lum which is visible from the parking area. The chimneys date from the 1920s and 30s and were used by road menders who would have erected temporary walls on three sides to create a short-term shelter, and a warm resting place at night.

Part of Glenlivet Estate, Tomintoul is recommended as a **Dark Sky Discovery Site**, and stargazers should head to the Field of Hope for great views of the Milky Way and meteor showers. The Field of Hope is about 450 metres north-east of Tomintoul, at the junction of the A939 and B9008. Access is free, and suitable for wheelchair users: the site itself is a small parking area with a hard-standing surface. From August to April, monthly official observation events are run here by the Tomintoul & Glenlivet Dark Skies Project, and the Glenlivet Estate ranger service. Throughout the year there are webinars and locally held public talks.

The **Tomintoul Highland Games** have been held on the third Saturday in July for over 175 years. The Games start at 11am and include traditional shows of strength including caber-tossing and hammer-throwing. Look out for the heavy-weight competitors wearing special cleats on the toes of their shoes: these metal spikes give them greater purchase when throwing. Just before midday a pipe band leads a procession through the village up to the public park, and throughout the day there are competitions for pipers, drummers, and Scottish Highland dancers. Fun competitions include trying to push an empty whisky barrel up a hill using only a broom handle.

The Cabrach and the Cairngorms

The Cabrach (🌐cabrachtrust.org) is a hauntingly beautiful, and remote part of Scotland which extends from the countryside outside of Dufftown and Keith in Moray, down to the edge of the Cairngorms National Park, and east into Banffshire.

Over a hundred illegal whisky stills used to operate in this region and smuggling was a well-organised activity. Plans to celebrate this history are under way. A heritage centre and working historic distillery which will use whisky making techniques from the 1800s are expected to open in 2024. This unique visitor experience is to be housed in the Inverharrochs Steading and will be a welcome addition to Moray's tourist attractions. Plans include The Cabrach Discovery Trails – a series of walks with interpretation boards and art installations.

The Grouse Inn (AB54 5EL ☎01466 702200) is as well-known for its well-stocked whisky bar as it is for warm hospitality and home-cooking. About eight miles south-east of Dufftown on the A941, driving across The Cabrach to the Grouse Inn gives you the opportunity to embrace the feeling of isolation in breath-taking wilderness. The Grouse is open daily from Easter to the end of October.

As you arrive at the northern edge of the village of Tomnavoulin, a large granite boulder bearing the image of a mighty golden eagle clutching a fish in its talons lets you know you are now in the **Cairngorms National Park**. The largest national park in the British Isles crosses five different regions including Moray, encompassing the Glenlivet Estate and Tomintoul within its borders. Spectacular scenery surrounds you in this famous park.

The Cairngorm Mountains lie at the heart of the park, but they are not the only range. In the north-west, the Monadhliath Mountains give rise to Scotland's longest river, the Spey, and are separated from the Cairngorms by the Strathspey Valley. To the southwest are the Grampian Mountains, which extend beyond the boundary of the park to Fort William, and Britain's highest peak Ben Nevis.

Ben Avon is the most easterly mountain in the Cairngorm range. A sprawling mass of a mountain, it covers more than 11.5miles^2 (30km^2), spreading from Moray into Aberdeenshire. The summit plateau is dominated by impressive granite tors, one of which forms the true summit and you need to scramble up this topmost tor to bag your Munro. Tomintoul is considered the gateway town if you wish to bag the mountain. A 25 mile walk via Strath Avon to a hight over 3000ft, it is a serious undertaking, with weather conditions which can potentially be arctic at any time of year.

EAST MORAY

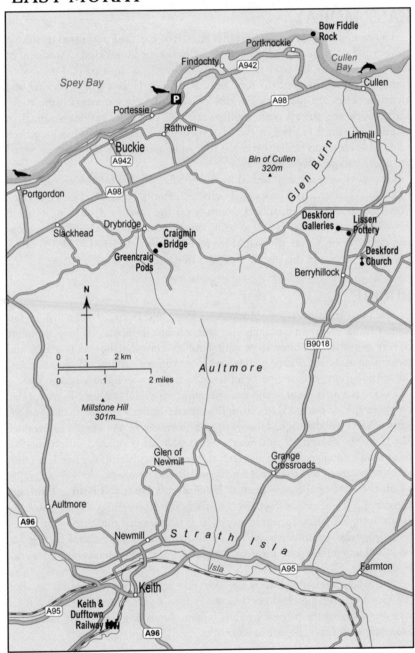

Bow Fiddle Rock

Portknockie

Findochty

A942

Cullen Bay

Cullen

Spey Bay

Portessie

P

Rathven

Lintmill

Buckie

A942

Bin of Cullen
320m

Glen Burn

A98

Portgordon

A98

Drybridge

Deskford
Galleries

Lissen
Pottery

Slackhead

Craigmin
Bridge

Deskford
Church

Greencraig
Pods

Berryhillock

N

B9018

0   1   2 km

0   1   2 miles

Aultmore

Millstone Hill
301m

Glen of
Newmill

Grange
Crossroads

Aultmore

A96

Newmill

Strath Isla

Isla

A95

Farmton

Keith

Keith &
Dufftown
Railway

A95

A96

EAST MORAY

The east part of Moray is a beautiful stretch of coastline populated by fishing villages full of heritage and backed up by rich agricultural lands. A colony of seals can regularly be seen relaxing on the beach at the east of Portgordon Harbour, or on Craigenroan rock near Strathlene House where parking and picnic benches are plentiful. Pockets of sandy beaches punctuate the rocky cliffs which are strewn with wildflowers, and home to various seabirds in breeding season. Evidence of Pictish settlements show that this has long been a desirable area, and perhaps you can find some treasure of your own in one of the many antique shops in the area.

Coastal villages are well served by the 305 Stagecoach bus which runs from Elgin to Aberdeen with stops at Fochabers, Portgordon, Buckie, Findochty, Portknockie and Cullen. Inland, Keith is on the number 10 bus route from Aberdeen to Inverness, as well as being on the main railway line between these two cities. Moray Council's Dial M for Moray service (☎0300 1234565) offers a weekday service in the Buckie area, and in Keith.

BUCKIE

The third largest town in Moray after Elgin and Forres, Buckie has its fair share of fine Victorian buildings and independent shopping. Its long shoreline is very popular on sunny days with families enjoying the sandy areas, and swimming in the sea. Picnic benches with convenient parking are situated along the seaside route, offering peaceful spots to sit and watch the world go by.

Buckie has grown out of the amalgamation of several smaller villages located on either side of Buckie Burn, from Buckpool (formerly Nether Buckie) on the west, and Gordonsburgh, Ianstown, and Portessie in the east. The areas of Yardie on the shorefront, and Seatown behind it, are populated with traditional fisherman's cottages, built gable-end to the sea to withstand the harsh winters, and without the need for street names, just house numbers.

In the west of the new town is **Buckie and District Fishing Heritage Centre** (7 Cluny Place ☎01542 834702 🌐buckieheritage.org 🕐Mon-Fri 10am-4pm; Sat 10am-1pm free entry). This highly rated museum is staffed by knowledgeable volunteers, and full of informative exhibits about fishing and boat-building in Buckie. Easy parking and great home-bakes are an added bonus.

The modern town of Buckie began to take shape from the late 1700s when the Gordons of Cluny laid out a new town on a grid pattern. This new town was set out along the ridge above and behind the fishing stations of Yardie and Seatown, with Cluny Square at its centre.

The heart of Buckie is its harbour and there has been a fishing settlement here from the middle of the 17th century. In 1842 Buckie was a busy fishing port and its first significant harbour was built in 1843. This was replaced in 1855 by the town's first stone harbour at Nether Buckie which was partly funded by the Cluny Family: unfortunately, it tended to silt up and become unusable. Unused for about a century, the old harbour basin was eventually filled in, in the 1970s: it now forms Buckpool Harbour Park with a pebble beach and the original quartzite harbour walls remain completely intact. Buckpool Harbour is the official start of The Speyside Way.

Buckie is ideal for long seaside strolls, and independent shopping on the Victorian high street.

Cluny Harbour as it stands now was built in 1877, funded again by the Cluny Family, facilitated growth in the fishing and shipbuilding industries. The railway came to Buckie in 1866, and the town had extensive connections along the coast. The Moray Coast fishing industry was booming in the 1800s, and the welcome addition of the railways enabled new markets to be reached. By 1913, Buckie had the largest steam drifter fleet in Scotland and the town continued to be prosperous. In the 1950s, Charles Eckersley moved from Manchester to Buckie, and started trading as a fish merchant. Eckersley noticed that the fishing boats were discarding catches of shellfish including prawns and scallops, regarding them as economically useless – he built the internationally successful Moray Seafoods based on this.

In the 1960s fishing quotas were introduced to prevent over-fishing of certain species, and much of the fishing industry moved to the bigger harbours at Fraserburgh, Peterhead, and Aberdeen - but Buckie managed to keep its footing as one of the main points for the Scottish shellfish industry. Food processing remains an important industry as there are large fish factories and smoke houses around the harbour.

Until 2013, there had been up to three separate boatyards in Buckie. Thomson Yard 880-1986; Jones Buckie Shipyard 1916-1995; and The Buckie Shipyard (formerly Herd & Mackenzie, est. 1903) which repaired and refitted most of the RNLI lifeboats in the UK but went into receivership. The Buckie Shipyard was re-opened by Macduff Shipyards in 2016 who specialise in fishing boats, but also produce other quality commercial vessels.

Religion plays an important part in fishing communities, and over the years there have been at least ten churches, not to mention chapels and faith halls in Buckie. One of the most impressive is St Peter's Roman Catholic Church, known locally as *The Buckie Cathedral.* Although there are older Catholic places of worship locally, they are modest affairs – for example, St Ninian's Church, about 4 miles west at Tynet. St Ninian's is a clandestine church erected in 1755, built after the Reformation, at a time when Catholic worship was tolerated as long as it was discreet.

By 1829, restrictions were lifted and within 30 years St Peter's had been built. A large church in a prominent location, it has been built in 13th-century Gothic style, and the imposing west face of the building is based on the majestic ruins of Elgin Cathedral. With its unusual twin spires, the red sandstone church may have been built with the intention of being a cathedral: even the Banffshire Journal announced the 'Opening of a new Catholic Cathedral' in 1857, but it never achieved this status.

Buckie's financial success led to it gaining an enduring reputation along the coast. Quite often, the babies of Buckie are still taken for a stroll in a traditional Silver Cross pram, but it's the bonnets which really catch your eye. Beautiful hand-knitted or crocheted bonnets with loopy decoration, lace, and ribbon, are *the* accessory for babies: *'ye'll ken a Buckie bairn by its bonnet!'*

Food & Drink
Bijou by the Sea Great Eastern Road, Portessie ☎01542 833915 🖱pozzibijou.com

An all-day restaurant and coffee shop with panoramic views of the Moray Firth, Bijou enjoys a good reputation with local patrons. From a late breakfast to light lunch or main meal, Bijou also serves home-bakes, fresh seafood, and locally produced drinks to hungry patrons in a light and airy setting.

DESKFORD PARISH
Just three and a half miles south of Cullen, the parish of Deskford deserves a mention for a few reasons.

Lower Deskford is rich in Pictish remains, and the hills above it have an abundance of burial barrows and fort structures. In 1816 a ditch digger unearthed the remains of a carnyx (a Pictish trumpet), the remains of which are now housed in the National Museum of Scotland, whilst a replica can be seen at Banff Museum. A full working version has been made and a clip of it being played is on the National Museum website. Excavations in 1990 showed that the carynx ended its life as a sacrifice - a votive offering.

A roofless ruin, the **Old Church of St John** at Kirkton of Deskford is little more than its external walls but preserved within these walls, is what is considered to be the finest sacrament house in Scotland. Set into the wall of the 16th-century church, is a recess where the sacramental bread would have been displayed in a special vessel call a monstrance. In the northeast of Scotland, the recesses were elaborately decorated. Recently restored, and preserved from the elements behind a screen, it is easy to appreciate skill of the craftsmen who carved the stone in 1551. The housing is decorated with intricately detailed angels holding a monstrance, and shields relating to the Ogilvy family who donated it to the church.

The old churchyard has several interesting memorials including a traditional looking stone which has been framed in an ornamental iron case, and the log-styled headstone of the Lawrence family which can be seen in other graveyards in the local area.

There had been a 14th-century castle, with a tower 70ft (21m) high associated with the site. All that remains of the castle is a private residence called the Muckle Hoose, and the walls of the tower which were reduced to 20ft (6m) to protect the church.

Ardoch Mill on the B9018 road (&01542 840037) is home to two craft businesses: **South Lissens Pottery**, and **SilkArt**. The light and airy mill has been transformed into a showroom for hand-thrown pots and mixed media artwork: delicate glazes evoke colours from the land and the sea on pieces of domestic ware that are surely too good to use, whilst desirable hand-painted fabric lampshades and wall art are just the thing to brighten your home. There's also a range of outdoor items including garden pots and bird feeders.

Follow the country track next to the pottery and where it ends, you will discover the expansive **Deskford Garden Galleries** (&01542 841400 fDeskfordGardenGalleries) and **Willows Tea Room**. A popular spot with locals, this old fashioned bistro celebrates times gone by, serving fine loose-leaf tea and dainty cakes on chintzy china, with white linen tablecloths, and some vintage tunes on the stereo. The tea rooms are accompanied by a variety of out-buildings dotted around three acres of natural gardens ornamented with artistic flair. Within the buildings you can find a wide selection of antiques, vintage designer clothing, crafts, and collectibles.

DRYBRIDGE

A peaceful hamlet surrounded by woods and farmland, Drybridge is just a three mile drive from the centre of Buckie. From 1884 to 1915, the Keith to Portessie section of the Highland Railway Line crossed the road at the village of Drybridge by means of a skewed-arch railway bridge. Although the line was never re-opened, the bridge remains and Drybridge is framed by this skilful piece of engineering.

There are some lovely walks around Drybridge, and you might want to explore the Laird's Way (⌂morayways.org.uk). This fully signed walk of 4.5 miles actually starts in Buckie, but you can do it in a loop of about 3.5 miles passing by Buckie at Linzee Park and continuing back to Drybridge.

Craigmin Bridge

A visit to nearby **Craigmin Bridge** is recommended. Parking is not possible at the bridge itself, but in Drybridge you should be able to park opposite the old Smithy, a category C listed building from about 1870, with an arched double-doorway, and a roof which is half red corrugated iron, and half slate.

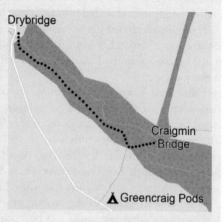

With the smiddy behind you, and a grassy area in front, look for a trail heading into the trees on the right hand side, just as the road goes round the bend.

A pleasant walk of less than half a mile through the trees will take you the unusual and picturesque bridge.

Craigmin Bridge is in the grounds of the Georgian mansion, Letterfourie House, which was home to two bachelor brothers of the Gordon family from 1774. The house is privately owned but access to the bridge is granted under Scottish Law.

The category A-listed bridge crosses the Burn of Letterfourie and your first view of it will be the unusual wave architecture of the side walls. Once you are across the bridge, a steep path on your right will take you down to the burn where you will be able to see the bridge from below. It might be advisable to wear wellies for this short walk, but the unusual architecture is worth the visit.

Not much is known about the bridge. Some people suggest it is two bridges built at different times: an initial footbridge, and the upper section having been added later in order to accommodate a horse and carriage. We do know that it was once the main carriageway leading to Letterfourie House. There is a small room built into each level of the bridge, another unusual feature.

The walk will take you past Inchgower Distillery which isn't usually open to the public, but they have been known to take part in the Spirit of Speyside Festival. The distillery is owned by Diageo, and uses unpeated malt from Burghead Maltings, and water from the Mindip Burn which originates in the Menduff Hills, to produce a variety of lower-Speyside whiskies. Most of the output ends up in Bell's – a well-known blended whisky.

If you are enjoying glamping at Greencraig Pods (Greencraig Farm, ⌨greencraig-pods.business.site ☎07734 355451) you will be able to join the woodland trail to the bridge through the gate at the bottom of the campsite.

FINDOCHTY

Locals pronounce the name of this colourful fishing port 'Fin-echty', where *ch* is the same as in loch and there has been a village here since the 1400s.

The village has grown up around a natural harbour known as Crooked Haven, which is watched over by the **White Mannie**, a war memorial designed by Correna Cowie in 1959.

Findochty was a busy fishing port in the 18th and 19th centuries, with as many as 140 boats docked there. When a new harbour opened at Buckie in 1855, much of the fishing fleet relocated, but you can still find more than a hundred boats at Findochty harbour today with a mix of fishing boats and pleasure craft lining the floating pontoons.

Painting the stonework on old houses in bright colours is something you will see in many villages along the Moray coastline, and Findochty is a particularly colourful village to visit. Sometimes just the large quoins and lintels around windows and doors are picked out in white; other times they are brightly coloured against a pale render over the

Relax in this pretty fishing village and enjoy some time on the beach.

walls. If the walls aren't rendered, then the mortar between the stones is highlighted and the result is very distinctive. It's not just homes that are painted: the Salvation Army building at Findochty looks very smart in its red and white livery.

Even the Church of Scotland here has been painted white and it is a shining beacon on the rocky bluff above the fishing community. Built in 1863, the congregation was called to worship by the sound of a fog-horn until a bell was installed fourteen years later.

Findochty has a charm of its own and offers little in the way of facilities for visitors, but it is precisely this no-frills approach that makes it a desirable location for a peaceful break, along with some of the best dolphin-watching opportunities along the Moray Firth. The Moray Coast Trail passes through the village, and a cliff-top path offers spectacular views as well as opportunities for spotting razorbills, kittiwakes, shags and guillemots – even eider.

Findochty Caravan Park (℡ 01542 835303 🖰 findochtycaravanpark.co.uk) is a small and friendly family-run site offering static caravans and pitches for tourers and camping. Tucked in below the hill, and just above a small rocky beach where rockpools wait to be discovered, you are almost certain of a fabulous sea view.

On the west of the harbour, beyond the church is Crooked Hythe, a small sandy beach, and on the other side of the headland curves Sandy Creek Beach with its share of both sand and rock pools.

In the village there is a shop and a chemist, and down by the harbour, a pub called The Admirals Inn (℡ 01542 832735 🖰 theadmiralsinn.co.uk) where you can enjoy a drink and live entertainment in the main bar, or a meal in the conservatory whilst watching the boats bobbing about.

A mile to the south is the ruin of 16th-century Findochty Castle which was built by the Gordons. It later passed to the Ogilvy family, before being acquired by the Ords in 1568. The Ord family was responsible for developing Findochty as a fishing port. The castle is on private land and cannot be accessed.

PORTKNOCKIE

Portknockie with its motto 'Aye Afloat' was founded in 1677 and like many other villages along the Moray Firth it was a significant fishing port in the 19th century. Although this is no longer the case, the harbour continues to be busy with small fishing vessels and private boats. Lobster creels are stacked along the harbour wall or stored in the crevice of the cliff, just as they would have been for hundreds of years. Safe within the harbour walls, is a small sandy beach with rockpools to explore and families can enjoy splashing in the bright blue paddling pool which was recently restored after a campaign by local residents.

Much of Portknockie is a conservation area and the oldest part of this cliff-top village is by the harbour where traditional fishermen's cottages are gable-end on to the sea, and close-built to give added protection from the elements. As the village prospered, larger houses were constructed with dormer windows, some of them still have steep stone steps running up the outside of the building to the roof - this would have provided access so fishing-nets could be dried and stored in the loft.

Stunning cliff formations are home to an abundance of seabirds.

The Station Hotel is a reminder that the railway used to run through Portknockie and although the trains ceased to operate in 1968, tourists can still cycle or walk the route of the old line to find themselves arriving in Cullen across an impressive viaduct.

The residents of Portknockie are rightly proud of their village and have created a series of leaflets to help visitors get the most out of their stay. Pop into the library to discover more about the village and its history, or any of the shops to get more information. The leaflets and suggested walks are also available online on the Portknockie website which is a wealth of information (✪portknockiewebsite.co.uk).

From the most northerly part of Patrol Street, a track runs out to the flattish headland. Known locally as Green Castle, this area has been excavated to show evidence of a fortified Pictish settlement. You will also find two large colourful fish embedded in the hillside. These mosaics which are a collaboration between local artist Geoff Roberts and the community, celebrate many elements of life in Portknockie.

This section of the Moray Coast has particularly stunning rock formations which are home to a great variety of birds in the nesting season. Visiting birdlife includes gannets (large seabirds with a distinctive yellow head), can be seen diving into the rich feeding waters.

The Moray Coast Trail skirts along the north of Portknockie and a small diversion to the left will take you scrambling down a dusty, worn track towards the impressive structure that is **Bow Fiddle Rock**. The Portknockie coastline has been carved by the crashing of the sea – caves, arches and stacks formed from the steeply folded Cullen quartzite provide dramatic habitats for colonies of seabirds. The world famous natural arch of Bow Fiddle Rock and the smaller Shitten Craig are home to fulmars, shags, and kittiwakes. Dumpy little razorbills appear to be 'falling with style' as they tumble from the cliff with their stumpy wings flapping wildly as they fly between the colonised rocks.

Explore further east to find a rock formation called Whale's Moo (mouth) which looks like a less eroded version of Bow Fiddle, and on a calm day, passage through it can be navigated with a small boat.

Jenny's Well is a natural spring which is now piped in order to retain it as a local feature. It is named for Janet Carstairs, a local woman who lived in a nearby cave in the early 1800s. During the 19th century, large crowds gathered at the well on the first Sunday in May to drink the waters which were said to give good health for the coming year. The hilly gully behind the well is packed with ferns which release a soft aniseed fragrance.

You may also find the Preacher's Cave: a large cave which has a long history as a meeting place and was known to have been used by 17th-century Covenanters, and then again in the 1840s by the Free Church when it broke with the Church of Scotland.

It is said, that to a native of Portknockie, each rock has a name and character peculiar to itself, and there are certainly a great many caves and rocks to explore. On the clifftops, a variety of wildflowers provides different habitats for several species of butterfly, whilst on the sand you may find a rare oysterplant (*Mertensia maritima*).

Sand Cheek, the western part of the sandy bay is considered a natural border between Portknockie and Cullen.

CULLEN

Cullen is known for both its beautiful location and rich history. Arrive in Cullen from the west, and you are likely to pass under the impressive eight-arched viaduct – unless you are cycling or travelling on foot from Portknockie, in which case you may find yourself enjoying views of Cullen from the viaduct itself, as it forms part of the Moray Cycle Way. You have the Countess of Seafield to thank for the views as she refused permission for the railway line to be built through the grounds of Cullen House. This viaduct is the largest of four such structures in Cullen which served the old railway line and frame this pretty, coastal town. Easily accessible on foot (take Grant Street from The Square, then head seawards on North Deskford Street), the viaduct will carry you west, high above the town and level with the clifftops.

Almost immediately after you ascend the ramp to the viaduct, you are on a stretch of grassy embankment which falls away with a sheer drop on the coastal side. Landside, you soon come upon a gravel path which will take you up the short, steep climb of **Castlehill**. Restored from a gorse covered wilderness in 2018 as part of a volunteer-led community project, Castlehill now features winding paths which take you up to the viewpoint at the top of a medieval earthwork. An information board contains comprehensive details about the archaeology and history of the site. Unfortunately, no trace of the actual castle remains, but you still get to enjoy the wonderful vista.

Back on the viaduct and heading westward, you are now on the Moray Coast Trail to Findochty. Enjoy panoramic views of the cliffs and beach ahead of you, and look back to see Cullen's Seatown being framed by the remarkable architecture of the viaducts. If you peer over the wall of the viaduct you should be able to see the Temple of Pomona – a garden folly in the gardens of Cullen House.

Cullen House is accessed both from a trail at the back of Castlehill, as well as along its main drive which opens onto Grant Street through a pair of handsome iron gates. Built in 1602, Cullen House is a historic country house which was converted into 14 separate private residences in the 1980s. The gardens of the estate are open to the public on Tuesdays and Fridays between 1.30pm and 4.30pm and form part of a pleasant walk to Cullen Old Kirk.

The Costa del Cullen will charm you with sandy beaches, characterful Seatown, and plenty of shopping.

Also accessible by car at the end of a single-track road, **Cullen Old Kirk** (Old Church Road, ƒcullenanddeskfordparishchurch) has been serving the community since 1573. Although there are mentions of a church on this site as far back as 1236, it is unclear whether any part of the current building is from that period. The medieval kirk is known for its fine stone carvings, in particular the ornate tomb of Sir Alexander Ogilvy (d.1554), Laird of Findlater and key benefactor of the church. Ogilvy is immortalised clad in armour, recumbent below an intricate Gothic canopy which encloses weeping angels and memento mori. An ornate sacrament house donated by Ogilvy is set into the wall by the side of his tomb and is not dissimilar to another even more elaborate sacrament house at the ruins of Deskford Old Parish Church.

In 1327, Queen Elizabeth de Burgh (second wife of Robert the Bruce) died at Cullen Castle. Her body was prepared for embalming and burial in Dunfermline, and her organs were buried at Cullen Old Kirk.

Of further interest inside the church are several more tombs, graffiti etched in the pews, and the imposing Laird's Loft from 1602. The church is often open for guided tours several days a week, please check their social media for more information.

At one time, the kirk would have stood at the centre of the original burgh of Cullen and the old town would have stretched along one long street from near Castle Hill to the Old Mill. South of the kirk would have been a mercat cross, tolbooth, school and homes enough to support a thriving weaving industry. The Earl of Seafield wished for more parkland and privacy and so, like the Duke of Gordon at Fochabers in 1776, he had the old settlement demolished in the 1820s (save for the church, and the Mercat cross which now stands in The Square), and commissioned the grander new town, on the popular grid-pattern, which rises up hill and inland.

The characterful fishing quarter of Seatown which nestles in the broad bay was already established with 29 homes in 1762 and benefitted greatly from the construction of the new Thomas Telford Harbour in 1817. Now, a couple of

Bin of Cullen 3.4miles (5.5km) 1hour 30mins

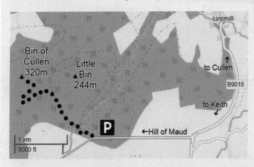

This bare, domed hill reaches its peak at 320m and can be accessed on several pathways.

Parking for this short walk is at a gated forest access track with a sign reading 'Seafield Estates – Do not Block the Entrance'. Please allow space for access.

The lower part of the bin is covered in pine forest and is a great habitat for red squirrels and crossbills. If you have the time and patience, you might even be rewarded with a sighting of a pine marten.

Follow the main track, ignoring a branch to the right. Continue on the main track, crossing a bridge over a burn.

At an intersection of trails, turn left, heading uphill past mature Scots pines. The route levels out for a bit. Turn left and continue climbing along a stony path. A sharp right will keep you zig-zagging up the hill.

The final 50 metres of the ascent sees the trees giving way to moorland, opening up wide panoramas with views as far as Lossiemouth, and across the Firth.

hundred houses in Seatown huddle together, end-on to the sea for protection. A colourful conservation area, many of the houses have their walls smooth rendered and distinctively painted, with the brick surrounds of doors and windows picked out in a contrasting shade.

Cullen Bay is perfect for open water swimming. The golden sands are ideal for building sandcastles, and rockpools provide excellent habitats for small sea creatures. Cullen Sea School (page 29) can help you get on the water with courses for stand-up paddleboards, kayaks and dinghy sailing.

When it comes to antiques, Seafield Street in Cullen is a shopper's delight. Work your way up from Trash & Treasure, and Cullen Collectibles to the old Seafield Church, which houses **Cullen Antiques Centre** – the largest antiques centre in the north-east of Scotland. Within the church building are specialist sellers of antiquarian books, jewellery, taxidermy, and Scottish collectables. The adjacent buildings are home to a stylish 'Salvage Yard,' which houses yet more unique retailers, a gallery, and a coffee house.

A favourite stop with many visitors to Cullen is **The Ice Cream Shop** for their award-winning home-made ice cream. It's not unusual to see people queuing down Seafield Street to get their hands on some delicious desserts. The friendly staff won't keep you waiting though – it's just down to how quickly you can choose from their tempting flavours and huge selection of old-fashioned sweets.

If you decide to explore the seafront east along Port Long Road you will come to Cullen Pet Cemetery, a touching resting place for beloved furry companions.

With panoramic views over the Moray Firth, Cullen Bay Holiday Park (Logie Drive ☎01542 840766 ⌨haugtonhouse.co.uk/cullen) is a friendly, family-run park which offers four-star static caravan holiday homes just a ten minute walk from the town centre.

Nelson's Seat is located a short walk from the caravan park and offers superb views all along the coast. At the entrance to the caravan park, a gravel path follows the eastern boundary wall of the cemetery and skirts the edge of the caravan park. When you reach a junction, take the path to the left, following the sign for Nelson's Seat. At the viewpoint an orientation map indicates some of the sights including the conical dome of Mount Morven, 55 miles away on the north coast of the firth.

Nelson's Seat is the last landmark on the eastern boundary of Moray. Beyond the Moray border, the ruins of Findlater Castle perch precariously on the cliff, and the beach at Sandend offers opportunities for surfboarding and windsurfing.

For further information, and maps of walks in and around Cullen including the Old Kirk, visit ⌨discovercullen.com and follow the 'information' menu.

KEITH

The gateway to the Malt Whisky Trail, Keith is a small, friendly agricultural town which prides itself on its heritage of the Scots language. Keith was awarded the status of the first 'Scots Toun' in 2014, as the residents have been actively promoting the use of Scots throughout the community: in schools, shops, and with Keith Community Radio which is on air from 6pm until 11pm every night. Tune in to 107.7FM and immerse yourself in the broad-tongued broadcasts from local presenters.

Nestled in the Isla Valley, Keith is comprised of Fife Keith on the west of the River Isla, and Old Keith and New Keith on the east. Old Keith dates from the 12th century and was used by the abbots of Kinloss as a centre for agriculture and distilling. The River Isla could be forded at Old Keith, and this accessibility resulted in the week-long Great Simmereve Fair where traders would arrive in Keith from as far as Glasgow and Orkney to trade in cattle and horses.

Keith is home to picturesque Strathisla, the world's oldest working distillery.

In 1609 Thomas Murray and his wife paid for the construction of a single arch packhorse bridge across the Isla. The **Auld Brig** still stands as a footbridge and is the oldest dated bridge in Moray. Traffic between the two regions now uses the Union Bridge built in 1770 which crosses the Isla above a pool called 'Guan's Pot' where women were drowned as witches.

New Keith was set out on the grid layout in the 1750s by the Earl of Findlater. Three parallel streets (Moss Street, Mid Street, and Land Street) are interconnected by a remarkable series of previously un-named narrow lanes. The lanes were known by various names over the years, indicative of a particular shop or a shopkeeper until 2013, when it was decided to assign names reflective of Keith's heritage and the use of Doric.

Fife Keith, founded in 1817 by the Earl of Fife in direct competition to New Keith, was also set out on the grid system. The Earl of Fife's planned village didn't have the same economic success as Findlater's Keith, and the two villages eventually combined.

In New Keith, the cottage industry of spinning and weaving was a success and led to the creation of large scale woollen mills, including the Isla Bank Mills which was a centre for the tweed industry and only closed in the 1990s.

It seems only natural that off the back of all this weaving, Keith should become a centre for kilt making, and in 1994 the Keith Kilt School was established to help workers who were being made redundant from the local mills to learn a new skill. Re-named in 2005, the **Keith Kilt and Textile Centre** (147 Mid Street ☎01542 886846) offers the world's only Scottish accredited course in kilt making. Visitors can drop in to purchase beautiful gifts and stylish home accessories, many of which incorporate colourful tartans. Chairwoman Linda Gorn is passionate about kilts and tartans – so much so that she even designs her own range. *Keith* and *Shades of Banffshire*, and the brand new *Shades of Moray* tartan are available exclusively from the shop. The colours in the design represent aspects of local life, and *Shades of Moray* celebrates the resident dolphins using shades of grey, the shiny whisky stills with copper tones, white represents the surf of the Firth, and a hint of green denotes the forests

With four distilleries in the immediate vicinity, it's no wonder that Keith heralds the start of the Malt Whisky Trail. **Strathisla** is the oldest, continually working, legal distillery in Scotland. Now home to Chivas (⬤chivas.com), it has been in operation since 1786 and adults can book a variety of tours and tastings at this picturesque distillery with its pair of iconic cupolas.

More recently, Keith has joined the boom in craft beers with The Keith Brewery (⬤keithbrewery.co.uk). This no-nonsense brewery produces award-winning beers (including Snake Venom, the world's strongest beer), which are available in their shop at the **Spey Valley Brewery** (Malcolmburn AB55 6YB ⬤Mon - Fri, 10am-4pm).

As well as being a stop on the main Inverness to Aberdeen railway line, Keith is also a stop on the eleven mile long Scottish Heritage Railway which is run by **Keith & Dufftown Railway Association** (⬤keith-dufftown-railway.co.uk). The most northerly heritage railway in the UK, the KDRA began operating from Dufftown to Drummuir in 2000 and extended its route to include Keith the following year. The pretty little station near St Rufus Church in Old Keith is well stocked with souvenirs and books, and is open when the trains are operational, which generally is three times a day, on Friday, Saturday and Sunday, from April to the end of September with an adult ticket for a return journey priced at £11. Special journeys operate throughout the year including an autumn whisky special, a 1940s weekend, and the Santa Special.

You might wish to pay a quick visit to St Rufus Church whilst you are nearby. The main doorway into the nave (leading from the lobby at the east end) forms a rare war memorial.

In the summer, hikers on the Isla Way (⬤morayways.org.uk) from Dufftown to Keith can board the KDRA weekend service instead of taking the bus back to their starting point. Just shy of thirteen miles, the Isla Way passes eleven distilleries, of which two have visitor centres: Strathisla at Keith, and Glenfiddich at Dufftown. The route follows the river Isla and runs parallel with the heritage railway. It can be broken into three distinct sections using the stations on the KDRA: Keith to Drummuir, which is mostly on public roads and unsigned; Drummuir to Loch Park has trails which are suitable for all abilities; and Loch Park to Dufftown. The directions for the official trail are given from south to north.

As the train pulls out of Keith station, it climbs through a picturesque valley, with the River Isla winding its way below. The Auchindachy Station is now a private residence, and the train passes though without stopping. Towiemore Halt is next on the line: it is a request stop so be sure to advise train staff before you embark or call ahead should you wish to join the train at Towiemore. The Towiemore stop exists because the railway line once served the Towiemore Distillery. The distillery closed in 1930, the buildings are now owned by a steel processing company. From Towiemore Halt, the scenery changes from rolling farmland to tall pine forests.

Drummuir Station is overlooked by the extremely grand Drummuir Castle. Privately owned by Diageo (the drinks giant which owns many distilleries in the area), the castle was built in the mid-19th century by Admiral Archibald Duff who once owned the village of Hopeman. The stunning castle was built in the romantic Scottish Victorian style. The main body of the castle is four-storeys tall, featuring crenelated towers and turrets, whilst the luxurious interior features gold detailing. Some rooms feature the original wallpaper, and decorations with yet more gold. Drummuir Castle can be booked for private and corporate events, but the rest of us will just have to enjoy it from the outside as the walled gardens are open to the public.

The estate of Drummuir Castle includes Loch Park and there are a series of trails (several of which are wheelchair accessible) which help you explore the beautiful parklands of the estate which incorporates deciduous woodlands, a man-made trout loch, and a salmon hatchery. The local wildlife includes water voles and nesting ospreys.

Those alighting at Drummuir may also wish to visit Botriphnie Parish Church. This simple parish church was built in the 19th century and replaced the old parish church. Built in 1617, the roofless, ruinous walls of the old church still stand in the graveyard.

The oldest gravestone is dated 1667, and although many are the modest stones of simple crofters, a dozen or so stones contain interesting detail from Celtic crosses to memento mori.

Back on the train, the line runs between the shoreline of Loch Park, and the pine covered hillside. The journey into Dufftown takes passengers across the Fiddich Viaduct, and under the walls of Balvenie Castle before curving round behind the Glenfiddich Distillery and into the station.

Shopping opportunities in Keith centre around Mid Street but are not restricted to it. Pop into the award-winning **Boogie Woogie** café and gift shop (2 Regent Square ☎01542 888077 🌐boogiewoogieshop.com), and alongside mouth-watering meals (brioche French toast, with bacon and maple syrup), you will also find a gift shop stocked with locally made gifts, and beautiful clothes for ladies and children. If you arrive by ScotRail, you will find Boogie Woogie a 13 minute walk down Station Road, and a good first stop as the staff pride themselves on being able to share their local knowledge with visitors.

Another handy stop for visitors is **Mither Tongue** (165 Mid Street &01542 887917 🖐mithertongue.scot). In keeping with Keith's Scots Toun status, Mither Tongue is an award-winning shop selling books and gifts celebrating the Scots language and heritage. It also serves as a visitor information point helping people enjoy their visit.

Keith's own website (🖐inkeith.com) is a great resource. Follow their 'Days Out' link to access leaflets for no less than six walks discovering points of interest around the town, and venturing into the beautiful countryside and woodlands, as far as the pretty little Falls of Tarnash.

In June, Scottish music and verse are celebrated over three days as the **Traditional Music & Song Association Keith Festival** (86 Mid Street 🖐keithfestival.com) breaks out in song and performance all over town. For over 45 years, attendees to Keith TMSA Festival have been able to take part in workshops and dances and enjoy sessions by established performers on the folk music scene. Information about events, and tickets for ceilidhs can be obtained at the festival office.

The days of the Great Simmereve Fair are long gone. Today Keith hosts the **Keith County Show** (🖐keithshow.org.uk) over 2 days in August at Seafield Park. Keith Show was established in 1872, and it is the most important event in the calendar for Moray's agricultural community. With a long standing reputation for showcasing the best in livestock, food, and drink, alongside performances of highland dancing and musicianship, Keith Country Show is renowned for being one of the best, and friendliest shows in Scotland.

The show is held on a Sunday and a Monday with the former being the big family fun day. Thousands of people flock to Seafield Park to see the massed pipe bands and enjoy competitions including show-jumping. The parade of vintage cars and tractors is a favourite with visitors, but the organisers also try to ensure they have something new each year, from magic shows to adrenaline-fuelled motorbike stunt shows.

FESTIVALS

Many of the towns and villages throughout Moray hold gala festivals and community fun days throughout the summer. The listings below are for the larger events which attract many international visitors to the area.

JANUARY
The Burning of the Clavie Burghead's New Year fire festival at 6pm on the 11th (when the 11th falls on a Sunday, the Clavie will be held on the 10th)
APRIL
Forres Foot-Tapper: The 'Real' Ale Festival foottapper.co.uk

Spirit of Speyside Festival spiritofspeyside.com (late April-early May)
MAY
Gordon Castle Highland Games and Country Fair
gordoncastle.co.uk/highland-games
JUNE
Keith Festival keithfestival.com

Moray Walking & Outdoor Festival moraywalkingfestival.co.uk
JULY
Dufftown Highland Games dufftownhighlandgames.com

Forres Highland Games forreshighlandgames.com

Tomintoul Highland Games tomintoulhighlandgames.co.uk

Speyfest speyfest.com Fochabers' celebration of traditional music
AUGUST
Aberlour Strathspey Highland Games aberlourhighlandgames.co.uk

Keith Show keithshow.org.uk
SEPTEMBER
Dufftown Flower Show dufftownhorticulturalsociety.uk
OCTOBER
Dramathon thedramathon.com

Whisky Colours Festival whiskycoloursfestival.com

INDEX